THE
HISTORY
OF
ISSUES

# Gay Rights

THE
HISTORY
OF
ISSUES

# Gay Rights

Kate Burns, *Book Editor*

Bruce Glassman, *Vice President*
Bonnie Szumski, *Publisher*
Helen Cothran, *Managing Editor*

**GREENHAVEN PRESS**
*An imprint of Thomson Gale, a part of The Thomson Corporation*

**THOMSON**
™
**GALE**

Detroit • New York • San Francisco • San Diego • New Haven, Conn.
Waterville, Maine • London • Munich

© 2006 Thomson Gale, a part of The Thomson Corporation.

Thomson and Star Logo are trademarks and Gale and Greenhaven Press are registered trademarks used herein under license.

*For more information, contact*
Greenhaven Press
27500 Drake Rd.
Farmington Hills, MI 48331-3535
Or you can visit our Internet site at http://www.gale.com

Greenhaven Press anthologies primarily consist of previously published material taken from a variety of sources, including periodicals, books, scholarly journals, newspapers, government documents, and position papers from private and public organizations. These original sources are often edited for length and to ensure their accessibility for a young adult audience. The anthology editors also change the original titles of these works in order to clearly present the main thesis of each viewpoint and to explicitly indicate the opinion presented in the viewpoint. These alterations are made in consideration of both the reading and comprehension levels of a young adult audience. Every effort is made to ensure that Greenhaven Press accurately reflects the original intent of the authors included in this anthology.

Cover credit: © Hulton Archive by Getty Images. A participant in a Washington, D.C., gay rights march displays a handmade sign.

LIBRARY OF CONGRESS CATALOGING-IN-PUBLICATION DATA

Gay rights / Kate Burns, book editor.
    p. cm. — (History of issues)
Includes bibliographical references and index.
ISBN 0-7377-2867-1 (lib. : alk. paper)
    1. Gay rights—History. 2. Gay rights—United States—History. 3. Gay liberation movement—United States. 4. Gays—Legal status, laws, etc.—United States.
I. Burns, Kate, 1963– . II. Series.
HQ76.5.G39 2006
323.3'264'0973—dc22
                                                                2005046331

Printed in the United States of America

# Contents

## Chapter 1: Catalysts for the Gay Rights Movement

# Chapter 2: Gay Rights Activism

gay sexual activity causes AIDS. The journal accuses AIDS activities of perpetuating dangerous propaganda to gain acceptance for gays and lesbians.

# Chapter 3: Legal and Legislative Battles

in the 1990s inspires a surge in activism to prevent and punish hate crimes.

# *Foreword*

In the 1940s, at the height of the Holocaust, Jews struggled to create a nation of their own in Palestine, a region of the Middle East that at the time was controlled by Britain. The British had placed limits on Jewish immigration to Palestine, hampering efforts to provide refuge to Jews fleeing the Holocaust. In response to this and other British policies, an underground Jewish resistance group called Irgun began carrying out terrorist attacks against British targets in Palestine, including immigration, intelligence, and police offices. Most famously, the group bombed the King David Hotel in Jerusalem, the site of a British military headquarters. Although the British were warned well in advance of the attack, they failed to evacuate the building. As a result, ninety-one people were killed (including fifteen Jews) and forty-five were injured.

Early in the twentieth century, Ireland, which had long been under British rule, was split into two countries. The south, populated mostly by Catholics, eventually achieved independence and became the Republic of Ireland. Northern Ireland, mostly Protestant, remained under British control. Catholics in both the north and south opposed British control of the north, and the Irish Republican Army (IRA) sought unification of Ireland as an independent nation. In 1969, the IRA split into two factions. A new radical wing, the Provisional IRA, was created and soon undertook numerous terrorist bombings and killings throughout Northern Ireland, the Republic of Ireland, and even in England. One of its most notorious attacks was the 1974 bombing of a Birmingham, England, bar that killed nineteen people.

In the mid-1990s, an Islamic terrorist group called al Qaeda began carrying out terrorist attacks against American targets overseas. In communications to the media, the organization listed several complaints against the United States. It generally opposed all U.S. involvement and presence in the Middle East. It particularly objected to the presence of U.S. troops in Saudi Arabia, which is the home of several Islamic holy sites. And it strongly condemned the United States for supporting the nation of Israel, which it claimed was an oppressor of Muslims. In 1998 al Qaeda's leaders issued a fatwa (a religious legal statement) calling for Muslims to kill Americans. Al Qaeda acted on this order many times—most memorably on September 11, 2001, when it attacked the World Trade Center and the Pentagon, killing nearly three thousand people.

These three groups—Irgun, the Provisional IRA, and al Qaeda—have achieved varied results. Irgun's terror campaign contributed to Britain's decision to pull out of Palestine and to support the creation of Israel in 1948. The Provisional IRA's tactics kept pressure on the British, but they also alienated many would-be supporters of independence for Northern Ireland. Al Qaeda's attacks provoked a strong U.S. military response but did not lessen America's involvement in the Middle East nor weaken its support of Israel. Despite these different results, the means and goals of these groups were similar. Although they emerged in different parts of the world during different eras and in support of different causes, all three had one thing in common: They all used clandestine violence to undermine a government they deemed oppressive or illegitimate.

The destruction of oppressive governments is not the only goal of terrorism. For example, terror is also used to minimize dissent in totalitarian regimes and to promote extreme ideologies. However, throughout history the motivations of terrorists have been remarkably similar, proving the old adage that "the more things change, the more they remain the same." Arguments for and against terrorism thus boil down to the same set of universal arguments regardless of the age: Some argue that terrorism is justified to change (or, in the case of state terror, to maintain) the prevailing political order; others respond that terrorism is inhumane and unacceptable under any circumstances. These basic views transcend time and place. Similar fundamental arguments apply to other controversial social issues. For instance, arguments over the death penalty have always featured competing views of justice. Scholars cite biblical texts to claim that a person who takes a life must forfeit his or her life, while others cite religious doctrine to support their view that only God can take a human life. These arguments have remained essentially the same throughout the centuries. Likewise, the debate over euthanasia has persisted throughout the history of Western civilization. Supporters argue that it is compassionate to end the suffering of the dying by hastening their impending death; opponents insist that it is society's duty to make the dying as comfortable as possible as death takes its natural course.

Greenhaven Press's The History of Issues series illustrates this constancy of arguments surrounding major social issues. Each volume in the series focuses on one issue—including terrorism, the death penalty, and euthanasia—and examines how the debates have both evolved and remained essentially the same over the years. Primary documents such as newspaper articles, speeches, and government reports illuminate historical developments and offer perspectives from throughout history. Secondary sources provide overviews and commentaries from a more contemporary perspective. An introduction begins each anthology and supplies essential context and background. An annotated table of contents, chronology, and index allow for easy reference, and a bibliography and list of organizations to contact point to additional sources of information on the book's topic. With these features, The History of Issues series permits readers to glimpse both the historical and contemporary dimensions of humanity's most pressing and controversial social issues.

# *Introduction*

M ost historians locate the beginning of the American gay and lesbian rights movement in the late 1950s, when homophile groups such as the Mattachine Society and the Daughters of Bilitis attracted enough members to garner national attention. The nascent movement then transformed into the gay liberation movement, which replaced the tentative and assimilationist strategies of the early homophile organizations with more radical political protests. The new spirit was symbolized in what has been called "the Boston Tea Party of the gay movement,"[1] when in 1969 patrons of a New York gay bar, the Stonewall Inn, refused to be victimized by police harassment. However, viewing the homophile organizations and their subsequent transformation into gay liberation groups as the beginning of the gay rights movement ignores two key developments without which the movement would not have been possible.

The first development occurred as a result of sexologists' work in the 1800s. These researchers claimed that homosexuals suffered from "gender inversion." In other words, homosexuals felt that they belonged to the opposite sex. This was the first time that homosexuals were considered to be part of a group. The second event was World War II, which provided avenues for gays and lesbians to meet, fostering a new sense of community. These developments led to the group identity that would make the formal gay rights organizations possible. Examining the long history of oppression against homosexuals makes clear that without a group identity that enabled the development of an organized movement, gays and lesbians would not have been able to fight successfully for equal treatment under the law.

# A Long History of Oppression

Historians have shown that prejudice against homosexuals has existed in many time periods and in many cultures. Some of the earliest recorded instances of antihomosexual laws were the ancient Hebrew restrictions against anal intercourse between men. There is no known evidence that other ancient cultures condemned same-sex relations, and some, like the Assyrians, included homosexual rites in their religious practices. When Christianity emerged, attitudes toward homosexual acts remained largely ambiguous until Christian canonical law was revised under the influence of Thomas Aquinas in the thirteenth century. Aquinas, in his *Summa Theologiae*, unequivocally condemned same-sex love as an unnatural vice and a heinous sin: "Copulation with an undue sex, male with male, or female with female, . . . is called the vice of sodomy. . . . [And] since by the unnatural vices man transgresses that which has been determined by nature with regard to the use of venereal actions, it follows that in this matter this sin is the gravest of all."[2] Prejudice against homosexuality was encouraged by the powerful Catholic Church, which preached against homosexual activities for centuries and significantly influenced European attitudes toward homosexuality.

## Homophobia in America

Not surprisingly, European immigrants brought their prejudice against homosexuality to the American colonies in the seventeenth century. Puritan ministers warned against the dangerous "sin of Sodom." Antihomosexual laws were justified by early American biblical interpretations, as historian John D'Emilio explains: "In Connecticut, the wording [of one statute] was taken from *Leviticus* 20:13: If a man also lie with mankind, as he lieth with a woman, both of them have committed an abomination: they shall surely be put to death; their blood shall be put upon them. The statute remained so worded until the 1820s."[3] In every colony sodomy was a capital offense, and the executions of at least five men were recorded. When citizens formed the United States of America, punishments for homosexuality began to soften in most states over time. While North Carolina kept the death penalty for sodomy until 1869, other states reduced the sentence to whippings and fines. Sexual acts such as adultery and fornication also were punished, but homosexual offenses were given especially harsh penalties.

In the early twentieth century a few urban enclaves offered some protection for gays and lesbians. One such place was the New York neighborhood of Harlem, when jazz culture was at its height in the 1920s. The bohemian atmosphere of the speakeasies and cabarets encouraged toleration, and occasionally even celebration, of gay culture. By the 1930s, however, the social climate turned increasingly against acceptance of homosexuality. Establishments friendly to gays and lesbians became the targets of police crackdowns and public scorn. A particularly strident article came out in the December 1936 issue of *Current Psychology and Psychoanalysis* about Greenwich Village, another New York district known for its many gay and lesbian residents. The author describes the village as "infamous for the past few years as the meeting place of exhibitionists and degenerates of all types." The author goes on to say:

> Sight-seers from all parts of the city made pilgrimages to view these misfits on parade. . . . Greenwich Village . . . is now a roped-off section of what showmen would call "Freak Exhibits.". . . Many of these creatures are actually paid for displaying themselves in night clubs to sensation-hungry guests. They revel in their own peculiarities, and are never so happy as when they have a good audience. They are possessed by one craving: to be noticed. They have never grown up.[4]

The article marked the beginning of a period when the psychiatric profession renewed its study of homosexuality, concluding that it was a severe mental illness. When the American Psychiatric Association issued its first official catalogue of mental disorders in 1952—*The Diagnostic and Statistical Manual, Mental Disorders (DSM-I)*—it listed homosexuality among the sociopathic personality disturbances. Psychology's view of homosexuality as a mental disorder also prompted the military to purge gay and lesbian soldiers from its ranks during and after World War II. It also fueled the Nazi persecution of homosexuals in concentration camps. After the war, Senator Joseph McCarthy launched an antihomosexual campaign; he accused gays and lesbians of being Communists and enemies of the state. From 1947 to 1950 more than five gays or lesbians were dismissed from civilian jobs each month. President Dwight D. Eisenhower issued a 1953 executive order that excluded anyone displaying "sexual perversion" from federal employment. His administration expelled an average of forty homosexuals a month from government positions.

## Historical Shifts Make Possible a Fight Against Oppression

Despite such a long history of prejudice against homosexuality, a mass movement for gay and lesbian rights did not get under way until the mid–twentieth century. Many scholars point out two important historical shifts that would make such a movement possible. The first shift happened in the late nineteenth century and the second shift occurred at the onset of World War II.

The first shift was the codification of sexual identity by nineteenth-century sexologists. Because the idea of sexual orientation is taken for granted in modern society, it is hard to imagine that people were not classified as homosexual or heterosexual throughout history. Yet in premodern societies such as ancient Greece and Rome, those who engaged in same-sex relations were not considered to be distinctly different from those who engaged in opposite-sex relations.

Ancient Greece is well known as the birthplace of democracy; it is also commonly seen as a society in which homosexuality was normalized. Many of the gods and goddesses worshipped by Greeks displayed homosexual tendencies, such as Zeus with Ganymede, Apollo with his various male lovers, and Diana with Camilla. The middle and upper classes celebrated love between men and boys as the premier romantic relationship. In contrast, heterosexual marriage was associated more with securing wealth and raising heirs than it was with erotic or idyllic love. The esteemed status of male homosexual love is clear from the way Greek citizens honored a specialized army of homosexual Lambda warriors who conquered neighboring lands. Moreover, marriages between men were officially recognized by the state in ancient Sparta and the Dorian island of Thera.

There is less evidence of widespread female homosexuality in Greece, in part because less attention was paid to recording the lives and activities of women, who were considered to be inferior to men. However, one lesbian received considerable attention, both as a lover of women and as a poet. Sappho, who lived around 600 B.C., was considered by her contemporaries to be one of the best poets in Greece. In her poems she openly celebrates love between women. Sappho's island home, Lesbos, eventually became the source for the word *lesbian*. Sappho's reputation as an exceptional poet continues to this day.

Homosexual love thrived in the Roman Empire as well. Same-sex marriage was legal and quite common. Romans did not see sexuality as an integral part of a person's identity. As in ancient Greece, whether someone preferred his or her own gender did not reflect on the way a person was perceived in society. People who loved someone of the same gender were not thought to be any more or less feminine or masculine, or any better or worse than those who loved the opposite gender. As biographer Plutarch wrote during the Roman Empire:

> The noble lover of beauty engages in love wherever he
> sees excellence and splendid natural endowment with-

out regard for any difference in physiological detail. The lover of human beauty [will] be fairly and equably disposed toward both sexes, instead of supposing that males and females are as different in the matter of love as they are in their clothes.[5]

Ultimately, neither the Greeks nor the Romans considered sexual preference of much interest at all. For them heterosexuals and homosexuals did not exist. Identity was organized around class status, political standing, gender, and whether a person was free or enslaved. Therefore, those who had relationships with partners of the same sex had no reason to see themselves as sharing important similarities with others in same-sex couplings. Sexuality was not a significant part of individual or group identity.

## Shift One: From Homosexual Acts to Homosexual Identity

Just as in ancient Greece and Rome, in Europe prior to the nineteenth century homosexual sex was seen in the context of behavior as opposed to identity: One engaged in homosexual acts but one was not a homosexual. Unlike ancient Greece and Rome, incidences of sodomy and other same-sex interactions were not accepted as normal; they were punished as isolated episodes of sinful or criminal behavior. However, those who were caught committing same-sex acts were not institutionalized as abnormal or belonging to a class of criminal people.

In Europe before the nineteenth century (and in non-European cultures throughout history), the homosexual-heterosexual binary was not the way that people understood their sexuality or their overall identity. In fact, the word *homosexual* did not appear in print until 1869, when it was coined by pamphleteer Karl Maria Kertbeny to protest sodomy laws in Prussia. The word caught on quickly, and other political pamphleteers repeated its use. Around this time, forensic scientists throughout Europe were developing a new discipline called sexology to study the sexual lives of people. They adopted Kertbeny's terminology and started scientifically classifying people as homosexual. Historian Matthew D. Johnson explains:

> The emergence of the term "homosexual" roughly coincided with these authorities' discovery of highly elaborated social networks of male persons in some European and North American cities. These men were typically understood to be effeminate in their appearance and demeanor, desiring and soliciting sexual contact exclusively with members of their own sex. By the close of the nineteenth century, these men came to be known to jurists and medical practitioners as "homosexuals."[6]

This new term expressed the growing conviction among psychiatrists and ordinary citizens alike that human beings possess a sexual essence that is central to their identity. By the mid–twentieth century, many in Western societies believed that there were basically two categories of human sexuality: homosexuality and heterosexuality.

The sexologists of the late nineteenth century claimed that homosexuals possessed two congenital qualities that differentiated them from heterosexuals: same-sex orientation and gender nonconformity. It was thought that homosexuals' desire for same-sex partners derived from a "gender inversion" that made them feel that they belonged in the body of the opposite sex.

This new concept of sexuality had both a positive and negative impact on homosexuals. By insisting that homosexuals were born into their sexual orientation, the sexologists opened the door for a more merciful attitude toward homosexuals in general. They argued that if homosexuals could not control their innate sexual orientation, then they should not be classified as criminals. However, homosexuals were still perceived to be abnormal and mentally unbalanced. Some efforts were made to stop the persecution of homosexuals, but those attempts were largely motivated by the idea that homosexuals were pitiful freaks. In any event, people who engaged in same-sex love began to see themselves as a persecuted group of people rather than as individuals who occasionally engaged in shameful acts. Thinking of themselves as homosexuals, they began to seek out others perceived to belong to the same group. Because they saw their disorder as congenital, they began to argue for the same rights as other "disabled" citizens.

## Shift Two: Minority Identity in the United States

World War II also provided the means by which homosexuals would develop a collective identity. The demand for soldiers in the military compelled thousands of young people to leave their hometowns and ship out to Europe or the Pacific Islands. Similarly, the war industry recruited thousands of workers to produce airplanes, weapons, tanks, and other wartime items. Even more workers were needed to fill all types of jobs left by those who volunteered for or were drafted into the armed forces. Throughout the war women found that they had access to employment that previously had been closed to them. Moreover, the conventions guiding military duties and workplace assignments often encouraged the separation of the genders. Men collected in boot camps and battalions. Women lined up together to fly transport planes or punch time cards in factories. Thus, wartime conditions offered men and women a unique opportunity to intermingle with a larger circle of same-gender associates than ever before.

For gays and lesbians the exposure to so many people gave them a better chance to meet others like themselves. It was the first opportunity for many to break out of the isolation they had experienced living on farms and in small towns. Away from their hometowns and families, gays and lesbians were able to build networks based on sexual orientation that provided romantic opportunities, fun and recreation, friendships, and mutual support. These relationships became the seeds for a gay subculture.

Preserving a sense of community was not easy for homosexuals when the war ended. Prewar heterosexual gender norms became entrenched again after the war. The nuclear family, built around the union of one man and one woman, became revered once again. Factories forced women out of the positions they had capably performed, for most thought that American industry owed good jobs to returning soldiers. These changes made it more difficult for gays and lesbians to meet one another and maintain social groups. These shifts also led to a return of overt hostility toward homosexuals, who were seen as a threat to the social conventions that were helping the nation return to normal after the war.

In spite of these changes, many gays and lesbians refused to relinquish the new sense of community they had discovered. They worked to maintain their networks and develop more cultural resources, such as gay bars, gay publications, and homosexual organizations. At the same time, Alfred Kinsey and a few other scientists and psychiatrists who were studying sexuality argued that homosexuality was much more prevalent in American society than ever before imagined. Evidence from their studies seemed to suggest that gays and lesbians made up a clear minority group in the United States. Gay and lesbian leaders used these findings to argue that homosexuals belonged to a subjugated minority group, no different than other minority groups working to win equal rights. A political consciousness spread throughout gay and lesbian networks. Leaders began to argue that gays and lesbians needed a civil rights movement of their own. By the 1960s groups such as the Los Angeles Gay Liberation Front (LAGLF) exemplified an era of empowerment from which there would be no turning back. The determination of these groups to mobilize the gay community is clear in this quote from the LAGLF:

> We shall go immediately and militantly to the defense of one another and any homosexual deprived of his right to a joyful, useful, and personal life. Street actions are now being organized, more will come; we shall not waste

our energies, however, on irrelevant issues. Our goal is—
*total liberation—life is for the living! We are alive! We want
all to be alive! . . . POWER TO THE PEOPLE!*[7]

Examining the evolution of gay and lesbian identity
shows that two pivotal periods in history were essential to
the establishment of the gay rights movement in the 1950s.
Sexologists in the nineteenth century argued that sexual
orientation is a core trait that defines the essence of human
beings. Under their influence, those who were attracted to
people of the same gender began to think of themselves as
homosexuals. Following this change in personal identity,
homosexuals had the opportunity to form communities
during World War II, when the crisis afforded them chances
to meet others like themselves and develop networks. For
the first time in history, gay men and lesbians could share
their stories and find like-minded friends and partners. The
common denominator that united homosexuals was the
persecution they experienced in a society largely hostile
to them. When gay men and lesbians shared their stories,
they began to consider themselves as an oppressed minority group in need of a rights movement of their own.

## Notes

1. Quoted in Neil Miller, *Out of the Past: Gay and Lesbian History from
   1869 to the Present.* New York: Vintage, 1995, p. 367.
2. St. Thomas Aquinas, *Summa Theologiae.* 1266–1273.
3. John D'Emilio, *Sexual Politics, Sexual Communities: The Making of a
   Homosexual Minority in the United States, 1940–1970.* Chicago: University of Chicago Press, 1983.
4. Quoted in Martin Duberman, *About Time.* New York: Meridian, 1991.
5. Quoted in John Boswell, "Revolutions, Universals, and Sexual Categories," *Hidden From History: Reclaiming the Gay and Lesbian Past,*
   ed. Martin Duberman, Martha Vicinus, and George Chauncey. New
   York: Meridian, 1989, p. 24.
6. Matthew D. Johnson, "Homosexuality," *GLBTQ: An Encyclopedia of
   Gay, Lesbian, Bisexual, Transgender, and Queer Culture.* www.glbtq.
   com/social-sciences/homosexuality.html.
7. Quoted in Will Roscoe, ed., *Radically Gay: Gay Liberation in the World
   of Its Founder Harry Hay.* Boston: Beacon, 1996, p. 178.

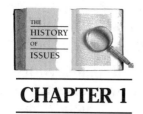

## CHAPTER 1

# Catalysts for the Gay Rights Movement

# Chapter Preface

S everal developments during the late nineteenth and early twentieth centuries provided catalysts for the gay rights movement. An acceptance of homosexuality within the arts and entertainment industry helped many gays and lesbians feel accepted, and a scientific report claiming homosexuality was more prevalent than previously thought prompted many gays and lesbians to feel more confident. At the same time, negative attitudes about homosexuals provoked increased resistance to discrimination against homosexuals.

One cultural arena that has been central to the advancement of many disenfranchised groups is that of art and entertainment. Gays and lesbians have benefited from the open-minded atmosphere present in many artistic communities in Europe and the United States. Whether in the literary salons of fin de siècle (end of the nineteenth century) Paris or Berlin, the jazz clubs of 1920s Harlem, or the intellectual circles of Bloomsbury in Britain, homosexuality was often tolerated, if not celebrated outright in artistic enclaves of the late nineteenth and early twentieth centuries. The relaxed moral codes observed by those communities allowed homosexuals to circulate more freely and express themselves more openly as members of a subculture.

Although art and science were positively impacting gays and lesbians, society in general continued to view homosexuality negatively. However, as discrimination against them increased, so also did resistance. For example, after finding a new sense of inclusion and purpose as soldiers and workers during the World War II effort, gays and lesbians then found themselves subject to military purges and civilian blacklisting. Heavily influenced by psychiatry's denigration of homosexuality as a mental illness, the armed forces developed the first official prohibitions against same-sex relations and discharged anyone suspected or caught in a homosexual act. Moreover, the growing anti-Communist fervor of the Cold War period following World War II linked homosexuals with other enemies of the state. Gays and lesbians were brought to testify before the House Un-American Activities Committee (HUAC) and often were branded as unemployable in their professions. While some gays and lesbians saw their lives destroyed by such persecution, others increased their commitment to fight the injustices they experienced.

Science, too, came to gays' and lesbians' aid during this period. One lone voice in the scientific community helped gays and lesbians by boldly calling public attention to homosexuality as one variety in a spectrum of sexual choices. Alfred Kinsey's research into male and female sexual behavior revealed that a much higher percentage of people engaged in homosexual acts than previously thought. The implication of his data was that homosexuality could hardly be unnatural or pathological if it is so prevalent. Gays and lesbians were emboldened by Kinsey's research to fight against discrimination.

During the late 1800s and early 1900s positive and negative developments combined to inspire gays and lesbians to begin fighting what they saw as injustices. These events were the genesis of the modern gay rights movement.

# Homosexuals in Uniform

*NEWSWEEK*

*During World War II the country needed thousands of military recruits and workers in the war industry. To meet the need many gays and lesbians left their farms, neighborhoods, and small towns along with thousands of heterosexual soldiers and laborers. Since soldiers and factory workers often lived in sex-segregated environments, homosexuals had more opportunities to meet others like themselves and build relationships and alliances. Those connections helped establish a gay and lesbian subculture.*

*During this time, military recruits were asked the question, "Are you homosexual?" for the first time. Notions of homosexuality in the 1940s stereotyped same-sex love as abnormal and dangerously associated with communism, which many believed threatened American security. Heightened anxiety about homosexuality influenced the armed forces to require soldiers to declare their sexual orientation at an induction physical examination. In the midst of these changes, little was said in the American media about the military's new policy toward homosexuality during World War II. The following selection is an exception. It appeared in* Newsweek *magazine on June 9, 1947, shortly after the army increased the consequences for soldiers discovered to be homosexual.*

Although Army regulations strictly forbade the drafting of homosexuals, scores of these inverts managed to

---

*Newsweek*, "Homosexuals in Uniform," June 9, 1947.

slip through induction centers during the second world war. Between 3,000 and 4,000 were discharged for this abnormality; others were released as neuropsychiatric cases. Last week [June 1947], with most of the records on homosexuals tabulated, Army medical officers, for the first time, summed up their strange story.

To screen out this undesirable soldier-material, psychiatrists in induction-station interviews tried to detect them (1) by their effeminate looks or behavior and (2) by repeating certain words from the homosexual vocabulary and watching for signs of recognition. In some instances, the urinary hormone secretion test showed a higher degree of estrogens (female hormones) than androgens (male hormones), just the opposite of a normal man. But this test was too uncertain and too expensive to try on every inductee.

Frequently, a latent homosexual, who had no knowledge of his predilection, was inducted into the service, only to develop alarming symptoms in camp and on the battlefield. Many of these men refused to admit homosexuality, even to themselves, and went to elaborate lengths to prove their masculinity. One of these ruses was regular and conspicuous absence without leave [AWOL], always with female companions. Often the soldier's primary trouble was not discovered until he was hauled before Army psychiatrists on an AWOL charge.

From case histories in Army files, these facts about homosexuals were gleaned:

- They topped the average soldier in intelligence, education, and rating. At least 10 per cent were college graduates: more than 50 per cent had finished high school. Only a handful were illiterate.
- Including all ages, there were more whites than Negroes in this group. They came mostly from the cities rather than the country.
- Although the majority had no family history of nervous or mental disease, many were from homes broken by divorce or separation. In many instances the

man had been brought up by his mother as a girl, or had been an only son in a large family of girls. About half assumed a "feminine" role, the other half "masculine." Most were either unmarried or had made a failure of marriage.

- As a whole, these men were law-abiding and hardworking. In spite of nervous, unstable, and often hysterical temperaments, they performed admirably as workers. Many tried to be good soldiers.

Once this abnormality was detected, the man was usually evacuated by the unit doctors to a general hospital where he received psychiatric treatment while a military board decided whether or not he was reclaimable. A good number begged to be cured, but doctors usually doubted their sincerity, and recommended discharge. At least half of the confirmed homosexuals, one psychiatrist estimated, were well-adjusted to their condition, and neither needed nor would respond to treatment. The majority, therefore, were released.

## The Blue Discharge

Early in the war, the homosexuals were sent up for court-martial, but in 1943–1944, the Army decided to separate most of them quietly with a "blue" discharge (neither honorable nor dishonorable) unless some other breach of military law had been committed. Last week, however, the Army announced a stiff new policy, effective July 1.

Instead of leaving the service with the vague and protective "blue" discharge, the homosexuals who had not been guilty of a definite offense would receive an "undesirable" discharge. A few of this group with outstanding combat records might receive an honorable discharge. Those found guilty of homosexual violence or of impairing the morals of minors would receive a "yellow" or dishonorable discharge.

# Homosexuality Is Prevalent

ALFRED KINSEY, WARDELL B. POMEROY,
AND CLYDE E. MARTIN

*In 1938 a scientist at Indiana University was asked to teach
the school's first course on the subject of marriage. When his
students asked him for information about sex, he scoured the
existing research for help, but what studies he found were
marred by a lack of evidence and scientific rigor. This inspired the scientist, Alfred Kinsey, to embark on a project that
would drastically alter Americans' understanding of sexuality. Enlisting the help of research assistants, he interviewed
over five thousand male subjects about every aspect of their
sexual history. The research culminated in the landmark
1948 publication of* Sexual Behavior in the Human Male,
*which quickly became a best seller.*

*Many of Kinsey's findings astonished readers, but the most
sensational of all were the statistics related to homosexuality. In this excerpt from what came to be called the Kinsey Report, the scientist reviews past studies that estimated as few
as one-tenth of 1 percent of men were homosexual. Kinsey's
data shocked the world when he found that 37 percent of
adult males had engaged in sex with another male. Kinsey
went on to research female sexuality and published* Sexual
Behavior of the Human Female. *His bold examination of sex
caused such controversy that he soon had trouble securing
the funding he needed to complete his extensive research
plans. Nevertheless, his research inspired many gays and les-*

Alfred Kinsey, Wardell B. Pomeroy, and Clyde E. Martin, *Sexual Behavior in the
Human Male*. Philadelphia: W.B. Saunders Company; Bloomington: Indiana University Press, 1948. Copyright © 1948 by W.B. Saunders Company. All rights reserved. Reproduced by permission of The Kinsey Institute for Research in Sex,
Gender, and Reproduction, Inc.

*bians to challenge the dominant view at the time that homosexuality was unnatural and abnormal. At the same time, those in the scientific and medical establishment who insisted that homosexuality was deviant attempted to discredit Kinsey's methods and conclusions.*

Many persons have recognized the importance of securing specific information on the incidence of the homosexual. The clinician needs to know how far the experience of his patient departs from norms for the remainder of the population. Counselors, teachers, clergymen, personnel officers, the administrators of institutions, social workers, law enforcement officers, and still others who are concerned with the direction of human behavior, may completely misinterpret the meaning of the homosexual experience in an individual's history, unless they understand the incidence and frequency of such activity in the population as a whole.

Administrators in prisons, mental institutions, public and private schools, colleges and universities, the Army and the Navy, Y.M.C.A. and scouting activities, and of all other sorts of groups, must understand the part which the homosexual plays in the life of the total male population, before they can understand the significance of the behavior of the particular individuals with whom they are called upon to deal. Scientific explanations of the origin and development of the homosexual, and, for that matter, of the heterosexual, will not be on any sound basis until we know the number of persons who are involved in each type of activity, the ages at which they first become involved, and the ages at which they are most frequently involved. There is no other aspect of human sexual activity about which it has been more important to have some precise knowledge of the incidences and frequencies.

There are many persons who believe the homosexual to be a rare phenomenon, a clinical curiosity, and something which one may never meet among the sorts of persons with whom he would associate. On the other hand, there are some clinicians and some persons who have had first-hand contacts in the homosexual, who have estimated that something between 50 and 100 per cent of the population has such experience.

There is undoubtedly a tendency on the part of some males who have had frequent homosexual contacts to exaggerate in their estimates. Some of these more promiscuous males have actually tested the responses of hundreds and sometimes of thousands of males whom they have invited to have homosexual relations. Many of them insist that a very high proportion of all the males whom they have approached have accepted such relations, and it is upon this fact that they base their opinion that most males are "homosexual" or that they are "partly homosexual," or that they "are really homosexual even though they may not be aware of it and may not have had actual experience." But they overlook the fact that the experienced male does not actually invite anyone to have sexual relations until he has had such social contact as may indicate the final success of his sexual approach. His contacts are, therefore, really confined to a very select portion of the males whom he meets.

## The Need for Scientific Evidence

Satisfactory incidence figures on the homosexual cannot be obtained by any technique short of a carefully planned population survey. The data should cover every segment of the total population. There is no other aspect of human sexual behavior where it is more fundamental that the sample be secured without any selection of cases which would bias the results. Many persons with homosexual experience very naturally hesitate to expose their histories. On the other hand, there are some who are so upset by personal conflicts or social difficulties that have developed out of their homosexual activities that they are anxious to discuss their problems with an investigator whom they have come to trust. In consequence, if one depends only upon volunteers in a survey, it is impossible to know whether homosexual histories are represented in an undue proportion, or less often than their actual incidence would demand. In order to secure data that have any relation to the reality, it is imperative that the cases be derived from as careful a distribution and stratification of the sample as the public opinion polls employ, or as we have employed in the present study.

Unfortunately, no previous attempts to assess the incidence of the homosexual have begun to satisfy these demands for statistical adequacy. The incidence figures which are most often quoted are derived from the 2 to 5 per cent estimate which Havelock Ellis made for England, and from the more elaborate calculations made by [Magnus] Hirschfeld, chiefly for Germany. The professional literature, if it does not cite these studies, rarely quotes any other sources except "the best informed students of the subject"; and through devious channels these data have become general property among people who have no idea of their origin. [Lewis M.] Terman and [Catherine Cox] Miles (1936) do credit a 4 per cent estimate to "the university medical staff in one of the largest of American universities." And there is a bare statement in [John] McPartland (1947) which reports a current "guess" that "the number of potential homosexuals in the United States is in the neighborhood of 8,000,000 or higher"—a figure that represents about 6 per cent of the total male and female population.

As for Ellis' estimate of a 2 to 5 per cent incidence figure for males, and double that figure for females, it is to be noted that this follows a review of the Hirschfeld data, and is made without any support other than the statement that "considering those individuals with whom I have been brought in contact by the ordinary circumstances of life . . . I am still led to the conclusions that . . . there must be a distinct percentage which may sometimes be . . . slightly over 2 per cent." As a matter of fact, Ellis never made any sort of systematic survey of any aspect of sex in any segment of the population. He had a minimum of face to face contact with his subjects, and depended largely upon information which was supplied him by correspondents. It is, of course, only a very select portion of the population that will send sex histories through the mails, and such histories are rarely more than partial accounts, usually of specific episodes that have been high lights in the life of the individual.

## Elaborate Studies

More elaborate attempts to obtain estimates of the extent of homosexual activity have been made by some of the Central European students. At the turn of the century, [L.S.A.M. von] Römer in Holland got 595 of his fellow students to give written answers to questions concerning their erotic reactions to females and to males. In 1903 and 1904, Magnus Hirschfeld conducted a much more extensive investigation.

Through the mails, Hirschfeld distributed forms to 3000 students at the Charlottenburg Institute of Technology, and to 5721 metal workers in Berlin, asking each recipient to indicate whether his "libido had always been directed only to females . . . only to males . . . or to both males and females." Of the 7481 persons who apparently received the letters, about 49 per cent answered. On the basis of these replies, Hirschfeld concluded that 94.3 per cent of the males were exclusively heterosexual, 2.3 per cent homosexual, and the remainder bisexual. The survey is open to the very severe criticism that it involved only a highly selected sample of the total population. What is more serious, one is left guessing as to the histories of the 51 per cent that failed to answer the questionnaire.

In a more elaborate attempt to secure estimates of the incidence of the homosexual, Hirschfeld contacted persons who, because they had homosexual histories, could supply some information concerning the extent of such activity in the business or professional groups in which they moved. Persons in the Army and Navy were asked to estimate how many in their whole company or among the officers in their group were known as homosexual. College students were asked to estimate how many of the men in their fraternities were known to have homosexual histories. Similar reports were obtained, from groups of Protestant clergymen and from Catholic priests, from postal employees, railroad employees, a group of court judges, bakers, bank employees, draftsmen, butchers, actors, hotel employees, the recorded histories of English kings, etc.—from a total of 34 different groups. Hirschfeld concluded that 525 out of the 23,771 persons in these groups were "homosexual." Calculations give an incidence figure of approximately 2.2 per cent, and this is the figure on which Hirschfeld subsequently depended.

## Science or Gossip?

Obviously this method of sampling falls far short of the demands of a scientific population analysis. It depends upon the ability of an informant to know the sexual histories of all the persons in a group, without collecting actual histories from any of them. It depends upon the informant's ability to recognize homosexual males (other than those with whom he has had actual contact) on the basis of their physical characters and mannerisms, or of their public reputations. Very often such reputations are nothing more than mere gossip. Moreover, there are many persons in any group whose homosexual histories are never known publicly. In brief, such sources of information are little better than the gossip and general impressions on which many persons depended before public opinion polls showed what can be accomplished in a statistically well-organized survey.

Hirschfeld deserves considerable credit for having tried on a larger scale than anyone had before to ascertain the facts on a matter that has always been difficult to survey.

Down to the beginning of the present study, no more serious attempt has been made. Nevertheless, the uncritical acceptance of these inadequate calculations has delayed the recognition of the magnitude of the medical, psychiatric, social, and legal problems involved in homosexuality, and delayed scientific interpretations of the bases of such behavior.

In later years, Hirschfeld had the opportunity to obtain the histories of persons who visited his Sex Institute at Berlin, some of them as patients, some of them merely as visitors who filled out the questionnaire supplied by the Institute. Some 10,000 of these were accumulated in the course of the years; but the data were uninterpretable because they were derived from such a select portion of the total population. Moreover, all of the Hirschfeld conclusions were biased by his opinion that a person is really homosexual only when his psychic or overt contacts are more or less exclusively so, and consequently his estimates may come nearer representing the incidence of certain degrees of homosexuality, rather than the totality of homosexual activity.

There have been other European studies that have been modelled on the Hirschfeld techniques, but all of them were based on smaller populations, and none of them has had as great influence on the thinking of clinicians.

## American Studies

In this country, three investigators have obtained data on the incidence of the homosexual in our American male population. It is notable that all three of them have secured figures which are remarkably higher than the European studies have given—not because there is any likelihood that the American picture is particularly different from that in Europe, out because all of these studies have come nearer satisfying the demands of a population survey. All of them involved a more thorough coverage of particular groups, and all of them were based on direct interviews with persons with whom the interviewer had had enough contact to have developed some rapport. [Gilbert Van Tassel] Hamilton (1929) found that 17 per cent of the hundred men in his study had had homosexual experience after they were eighteen years old. [Glenn V.] Ramsey (1943), in a study of 291 younger boys, one-half of whom constituted a hundred percent sample of a seventh and eighth grade group in a junior high school, found that 30 per cent had had adolescent homosexual experience to the point of orgasm. More recently (1947), [Frank W.] Finger has reported 27 per cent of a college class of 111 males admitting "at least one overt homosexual episode involving orgasm." These figures come remarkably close to those which we have obtained in the present study.

One other source of data on the extent of "homosexuality" among American males has recently become available through statistics gathered by Selective Service Boards and at induction centers during the last war [World War II]. Theoretically, this should have been a splendid opportunity to gain information that would have been of considerable scientific use and of considerable practical use to the armed forces. From these sources, the over-all figures show that about one-tenth of 1 per cent of all the men were rejected by draft boards, about 0.4 per cent were turned down at induction centers, and about as many more were subsequently discharged for homosexual activity while they were in active service. The total gives about 1 per cent officially identified as "homosexual." These figures are so much lower than any which case history studies have obtained that they need critical examination.

## Obvious Problems with Military Studies

The most obvious explanation of these very low figures lies in the fact that both the Army and Navy had precluded the possibility of getting accurate data on these matters by announcing at the beginning of the war that they intended to exclude all persons with homosexual histories. The American Army and Navy have always been traditionally opposed to homosexual activity, and in the last war, for the first time, they turned to psychiatrists to provide expert help in eliminating individuals with such histories.

Physicians on draft boards and psychiatrists at induction centers were charged with the responsibility of detecting and eliminating men with such records, and many of the psychiatrists at induction centers paid especial attention to identifying these men. While the reasons for elimination of any man were supposed to be kept confidential, they were in actuality not infrequently known to the whole community in which he lived. The mere fact that he was rejected under a particular classification, or discharged from the Army or Navy on a particular discharge form, often made him a subject for suspicion, and in a large number of instances practically precluded the possibility of his securing employment as a civilian. Consequently, few men with any common sense would admit their homosexual experience to draft boards or to psychiatrists at induction centers or in the services.

It is amazing that some of the psychiatrists . . . apparently believed that they were getting a true record under these circumstances. Only a naive individual, one who was badly neurotic and upset over his experience, or an effeminate type of male who freely exhibited his homosexual interests, was ordinarily detected through the official channels. Many of the psychiatrists were less experienced in identifying the obviously homosexual male than several million untrained persons who had had actual contact with homosexual activities. Many psychiatrists realized this, and some of them recognized the fact that the incidence of homosexual activity in the armed forces must have been high—even involving as many as 10 per cent or more of the men.

It is also to be noted that at induction centers the average interview was limited to less than three minutes. Considering that the psychoanalysts and many of the other psychiatrists have heretofore insisted that one could not expect to obtain data on socially taboo items of sexual behavior in anything less that a hundred hours of analysis, it is the more surprising that the results of these short interviews at induction centers should have been taken seriously.

Discharges from the Army and Navy similarly have not provided any adequate source of information on the actual incidence of homosexual activity. Many psychiatrists in the armed forces were aware of the great social damage done to an individual who was discharged for such reasons, and they considered it desirable to help him by showing flat feet, stomach ulcers, shock, or some other non-sexual item as the immediate cause of the discharge. Consequently, no one anywhere in official circles in the Army and the Navy will ever be able to obtain any adequate estimate of the number of men with homosexual activity who were identified and discharged from the services during the war.

The estimates on the incidence of the homosexual, range, then, from these Selective Service figures of one-tenth of 1 per cent to the 100 per cent estimates of some of the psychoanalysts and of some promiscuous homosexual males. It has, therefore, been especially important in our present study to apply all of the techniques of a statistically sound population survey to obtaining data on this particular matter.

## The Present Study

The statistics given throughout this [study] on the incidence of homosexual activity, and the statistics to be given in the present section of this chapter, are based on those persons who have had physical contacts with other males, and who were brought to orgasm as a result of such contacts. By any strict definition such contacts are homosexual, irrespective of the extent of the psychic stimulation involved, of the techniques employed, or of the relative importance of the homosexual and the heterosexual in the history of such an individual. These are not data on the number of persons who are "homosexual," but on the number of persons who have had at least some homosexual experience—even though sometimes not more than one experience—up to the ages shown in the tables and curves. The incidences of persons who have had various amounts of homosexual experience are presented in a later section of this chapter. . . .

In these terms (of physical contact to the point of orgasm), the data in the present study indicate that at least 37 per cent of the male population has some homosexual experience between the beginning of adolescence and old age. This is more than one male in three of the persons that one may meet as he passes along a city street. Among the males who remain unmarried until the age of 35, almost exactly 50 per cent have homosexual experience between the beginning of adolescence and that age. Some of these persons have but a single experience, and some of them have much more or even a lifetime of experience; but all of them have at least some experience to the point of orgasm.

These figures are, of course, considerably higher than any which have previously been estimated; . . . but they must be understatements, if they are anything other than the fact.

## Surprising Data

We ourselves were totally unprepared to find such incidence data when this research was originally undertaken. Over a period of several years we were repeatedly assailed with doubts as to whether we were getting a fair cross section of the total population or whether a selection of cases was biasing the results. It has been our experience, however, that each new group into which we have gone has provided substantially the same data. Whether the histories were taken in one large city or another, whether they were taken in large cities, in small towns, or in rural areas, whether they came from one college or from another, a church school or a state university or some private institution, whether they came from one part of the country or from another, the incidence data on the homosexual have been more or less the same. . . .

If we had arrived at the present incidence figures by a single calculation based on a single population, one might well question their validity. But the determination of the extent of the homosexual in the population is too important a matter to be settled on anything but an elaborately devised system of samples. When twelve ways of obtaining data give results that are as consistent . . . there can be no question that the actual incidence of the homosexual is at least 37 and 50 per cent. . . . The tests show that the actual figures may be as much as 5 per cent higher, or still higher.

Those who have been best acquainted with the extent of homosexual activity in the population, whether through clinical contacts with homosexual patients, through homosexual acquaintances, or through their own firsthand homosexual experience, will not find it too difficult to accept the accumulative incidence figures which are arrived at here. There are many who have been aware of the fact that persons with homosexual histories are to be found in every age group, in every social level, in every conceivable occupation, in cities and on farms, and in the most remote areas in the country. They have known the homosexual in young adolescents and in persons of every other age. They have known it in single persons and in the histories of males who were married. In large city communities they know that an experienced observer may identify hundreds of persons in a day whose homosexual interests are certain. They have known the homosexuality of many persons whose histories were utterly unknown to most of their friends and acquaintances. They have repeatedly had the experience of discovering homosexual histories among persons whom they had known for years before they realized that they had had anything except heterosexual experience.

On the other hand, the incidence of the homosexual is not 100 per cent, as some persons would have it. There is no doubt that there are males who have never been involved in any sexual contact with any other male, and who have never been conscious of any erotic arousal by another male. For while some of the psychoanalysts will contend to the contrary, it is to be pointed out that there are several dozen psychoanalysts who have contributed histories to this study who have insisted that they have never identified homosexual experience or reactions in their own histories. . . .

The active incidence figures are highest among single males of the high school level. In the late teens nearly every other male of this level (41%) is having some homosexual contact, and between the ages of 26 and 30 it is had by 46 per cent of the group. Among the males of the grade school level about 1 in 4 (22 to 27%) has any homosexual experience in any age period of the pre-marital years. Among the males who belong to the college level only about 1 in 5 has homosexual experience between adolescence [puberty] and 15 (22%), 1 in 6 (16%) has such relations in the later teens, and less than 1 in 10 (10%) has homosexual relations between the ages of 21 and 25. Among males who never go beyond grade school, about the same number of individuals is involved while they are actually in grade school, during their late teens when they are out of school, and in all the subsequent years until they marry. Among the males who stop their schooling at high school levels a larger number is involved after they have left school. For the males who belong to the college level, the largest number is involved while they are in high school, but the number steadily decreases in later years.

Homosexual activities occur in a much higher percentage of the males who became adolescent at an early age; and in a definitely smaller percentage of those who became adolescent at later ages. For instance, at the college level, during early adolescence about 28 per cent of the early-adolescent boys are involved, and only 14 per cent of the boys who were late in becoming adolescent. This difference is narrowed in successive age periods, but the boys who became adolescent first are more often involved even ten and fifteen years later. It is to be recalled that these early-adolescent boys are the same ones who have the highest incidences and frequencies in masturbation and in heterosexual contacts. It is the group which possesses on the whole the greatest sex drive, both in early adolescence and throughout most of the subsequent periods of their lives.

Homosexual activities occur less frequently among rural groups and more frequently among those who live in towns or cities. On the other hand, it has already been pointed out that this is a product not only of the greater opportunity which the city may provide for certain types of homosexual contacts, but also of the generally lower rate of total outlet among males raised on the farm. It has also been pointed out that in certain of the most remote rural areas there is considerable homosexual activity among lumbermen, cattlemen, prospectors, miners, hunters, and others engaged in out-of-door occupations. The homosexual activity rarely conflicts with their heterosexual relations, and is quite without the argot, physical manifestations, and other affectations so often found in urban groups. There is a minimum of personal disturbance or social conflict over such activity. It is the type of homosexual experience which the explorer and pioneer may have had in their histories.

On the whole, homosexual contacts occur most frequently among the males who are not particularly active in their church connections. They occur less frequently among devout Catholics, Orthodox Jewish groups, and Protestants who are active in the church. The differences are not always great, but lie constantly in the same direction.

Among married males the highest incidences of homosexual activity appear to occur between the ages of 16 and 25, when nearly 10 per cent of the total population of married males is involved. The available data seem to indicate that the percentage steadily drops with advancing age, but we have already suggested that these figures are probably unreliable. Younger, unmarried males have regularly given us some record of sexual contacts with older, married males.

Many married males with homosexual experience currently in their histories have, undoubtedly, avoided us, and it has usually been impossible to secure hundred per cent groups of older married males, especially from males of assured social position, primarily because of the extra-marital intercourse which they often have, and sometimes because some of them have active homosexual histories. About 10 per cent of the lower level married males have admitted homosexual experience between the ages of 16 and 20. About 13 per cent of the high school level has admitted such experience after marriage and between the ages of 21 and 25. Only 3 per cent of the married males of college level have admitted homosexual experience after marriage—mostly between the ages of 31 and 35. It has been impossible to calculate accumulative incidence figures for these several groups, but they must lie well above the active incidence figures just cited.

Finally, it should be noted that there is no evidence that the homosexual involves more males or, for that matter, fewer males today than it did among older generations, at least as far back as the specific record in the present study goes.

# The Kinsey Report Is Dangerous

EDMUND BERGLER

*The publication of Alfred Kinsey's 1948* Sexual Behavior in the Human Male, *popularly known as the Kinsey Report, ignited a furor of debate in the scientific and medical professions. Of particular interest were Kinsey's conclusions about homosexuality. His claim that homosexual experiences or feelings were common challenged the then-popular view that homosexuality is unnatural, pathological, and treatable. A handful of anthropologists and psychoanalysts vilified Kinsey, accusing him of shoddy research and of degrading American values. However, an investigation into his data by the American Statistical Association rated his research as the best ever done in the field.*

*The following selection articulates many of the objections that were raised by psychiatrists in reaction to the Kinsey Report. The selection's author, Edmund Bergler, was a prominent psychoanalyst who wrote volumes of material on homosexuality, often describing gays and lesbians as sick, spiteful, arrogant, and untrustworthy. In this review of Kinsey's work, he sets out to portray Kinsey as naive, incompetent, and dangerous to national security.*

Edmund Bergler, "Homosexuality and the Kinsey Report," in *The Homosexuals: As Seen by Themselves and Thirty Authorities*, ed. A.M. Krich. New York: The Citadel Press, 1968.

## "One Male in Three . . . Has Had Some Homosexual Experience"

[Scientist Alfred] Kinsey and his collaborators gathered their conclusions by questioning 12,000 people. I believe that Kinsey's figures are correctly compiled and presented in good faith. Still, his disregard for psychologic factors has very likely played a trick on him; he takes his human guinea pigs for idealists who volunteered only for the purpose of further scientific research:

"Thousands of persons have helped by contributing records of their own sexual activities, by interesting others in the research . . . Even the scientist seems to have underestimated the faith of the man of the street in the scientific method, his respect for the results of scientific research, and his confidence that his own life and the whole of the social organization will ultimately benefit from the accumulation of scientifically established data. . . . The chief appeal has been *altruistic. . . .*"

Kinsey himself has some doubts about his volunteers, however: "Still more remarkable is the fact that many of the case histories in the present study have come from subjects who agreed to give histories *within the first few minutes* after they first met the interviewer. *We are not sure that we completely comprehend why people have been willing to talk to us.*"

The chances are that many volunteers who secondarily interested other volunteers, though *consciously* inspired by noble intentions, had some less altruistic *unconscious* motives. Among these, one could suspect, were many homosexuals who gladly used the opportunity of proving, by volunteering, that "everybody" has homosexual tendencies—thus seeking to *diminish their own inner guilt.*

Moreover, the clinical fact remains that the circle of friends of neurotics consists almost exclusively of neurotics. Hence the second and third "crop" of volunteers must have consisted of too many neurotics, too.

I believe that Kinsey's figures about homosexual outlet

will be revised downward as the present 12,000 interrogated are increased to 100,000, as Kinsey promises in the next 20 years.

One could enlarge on the involuntary selectivity of Kinsey's material by enumerating other unconscious propelling factors in the interrogated persons—for instance, the fact that it sometimes takes trained psychiatrists months to get the facts out of the patient, whereas Kinsey and his collaborators get it in one interview. We "fire questions" no less than Kinsey's schedule provides for; still, we need more time. Strange—or someone seems to be naïve.

But even assuming the improbable fact that further interrogations will only confirm the published statistics, the complete neglect of unconscious factors renders the results dubious. . . .

## Homosexuality—Biologic Destiny or Neurotic Disease?

Kinsey pleads in effect for the acceptance of homosexuality as a biologically given fact to which law and prejudice had better adapt themselves. . . .

[Kinsey writes] "The evidence that we now have on the incidence and frequency of homosexual activity indicates that *at least a third of the male population would have to be isolated from the rest of the community, if all those with any homosexual capacities were to be so treated.* It means that at least 13 percent of the male population (rating 4 to 6 on the heterosexual-homosexual scale) would have to be institutionalized and isolated, if all persons who were predominantly homosexual were to be handled in that way. Since about 34 percent of the total population of the United States are adult males, this means that there are about six and a third million males in the country who would need such isolation."

Strangely enough, Kinsey sees only the antithesis: acceptance of homosexuality as a biologic fact vs. senseless segregation. He speaks disparagingly of treatment of homosexuality (he puts it ironically into quotation marks). The *third* possibility, namely to declare homosexuality a *neurotic disease*, does not even occur to him.

The facts are that the initial pessimism toward psychoanalytic treatment of homosexuals (maintained by psychoanalysts previously) is completely unjustified. Triumphantly Kinsey states:

"The opinion that homosexual activity in itself provides evidence of a psychopathic personality is materially challenged by these incidence and frequency data. Of the *40 or 50 percent of the male population which has homosexual experience*, certainly a high proportion would not be considered psychopathic personalities. . . . As a matter of fact, there is an increasing proportion of the most skilled psychiatrists who make no attempt to redirect behavior, but who devote their attention to helping an individual accept himself, and to conduct himself in such a manner that he does not come into open conflict with society."

Kinsey refers here to the outdated attempt, based on therapeutic helplessness, to reconcile a homosexual with his "destiny" by diminishing his guilt. The attempt is as outdated as treatment of syphilis before the therapeutic acceptance of salvarsan.

On the other hand, endocrinology has nothing therapeutic to contribute to the problem of homosexuality. This fact is best illustrated in the summary of a witty endocrinologist: "Some psychiatrists claim that the best they can do for a homosexual is to make an unhappy homosexual a 'happy' one. This is little, but still more than endocrinology can do for a homosexual: the latter can only make a prosperous homosexual a less prosperous one."

The most that can be said psychiatrically about the biologic substructure in homosexuality was summarized by P. Schilder:

"It has been repeatedly attempted to apply the results of [R.] Goldschmidt's experiments to the problem of homosexuality. His experiments deal with very definite physical characteristics, and to transfer his results to the psychic field has no scientific basis at the present time. As to the experiments of [Eugen] Steinach, who had feminized male guinea pigs which really behaved like females and were sought as females by males, it must be emphasized that there is no proof that in homosexuals changes in the hormones take place similar to those experimentally produced. I agree therefore with Oswald Schwarz that *no proof exists that homosexuality is due to biologic hermaphroditism.* . . . "

The fact remains that today homosexuality is a curable neurotic disease, requiring specific therapeutic techniques and prerequisites.

## Dangers of the Myth of a New National Disease

Let us do some figuring; after all, we are dealing with a statistical study.

According to Kinsey, people using the "homosexual outlet" comprise *"at least"* 37 percent of the male population of the United States. According to the last census, 34 percent of the total population are adult males. The last published report on the population of the United States is one released on March 10, 1948: The total population for 1947 was 145,340,000. Thirty-four percent of 145 million is approximately 49 million; hence there are 49 million adult males. From these "at least" 37 percent use the "homosexual outlet" part-time, full-time, or sometimes. Thirty-seven percent of 49 million is approximately 18 million. Hence there are 18 million people whom the unpsychological outer world (though against Kinsey's protests) would consider "homosexuals."

Add to these 16 and one-half millions the vast army of Lesbians—the number of which is statistically not yet determined, though frequently assumed (Magnus Hirschfeld) to *double* that of their male confreres. By simple arithmetic, one arrives at somewhere around *50 million people seated on the homosexual scale of the "heterosexual-homosexual balance."*

If these figures are only approximately correct (Kinsey sticks to percentages and does not translate them into actual numbers), then "the homosexual outlet" is *the predominant national disease* overshadowing in numbers cancer, tuberculosis, heart failure, infantile paralysis. Of course, Kinsey denies that the "homosexual outlet" is a disease in the first place. But psychiatrically, we are dealing with a disease, however you slice it.

Scientific research is interested in truth only, and can not be responsible for the possible misuse by the laity of these results. But what if the results are erroneous? Then actual damage—otherwise only a painful though unavoidable concomitant—is done for no purpose at all.

I believe that Kinsey's results on homosexuality will do damage without furthering the cause of scientific truth.

First, every homosexual will receive tax-free an "irrefutable," "statistical," and "scientific" argument for the maintenance and spread of his perversion without conscious guilt.

Second, "borderline cases" will be more easily persuaded to enter homosexual relations. The scruples of not a few candidates for homosexuality will be torn down by statistical proofs: "Who are you to argue with 37 percent of the male population?"

Third, many impotent neurotics, entirely innocent of the "homosexual outlet," will suffer, through a grotesque misunderstanding. Women have a simple formula: "Impotent, *ergo* a fairy." This, of course, is erroneous. There are dozens of unconscious reasons for psychogenic potency-disturbance, completely unrelated to homosexuality. Still, women cling stubbornly to this silly simplification. Taking into account the fact that men are ignorant on that score, too, men are apt to believe it. I know of cases in which irate wives have first put Jackson's *The Fall of Valor* (which endorses Kinsey's viewpoint in a literary way) on their husband's night tables, followed by Kinsey's book.

Fourth, every neurotic will, in cases of potency disturbance, immediately suspect "biologically conditioned" homosexuality, though his troubles actually have completely different (and unconscious) reasons. Since there are millions of neurotics and only infinitesimal possibilities of psychiatric help (due to lack of knowledge, money, trained psychiatrists) greater desperation among untreated neurotics will result.

Last but not least, Kinsey's erroneous psychological conclusions pertaining to homosexuality will be politically and propagandistically used against the United States abroad, stigmatizing the nation as a whole in a whisper campaign, especially since there are no comparative statistics available for other countries.

Kinsey attempts to give homosexuals a clean bill of health, and claims, rather emotionally:

"Males do not represent two discrete populations, homosexual and heterosexual. The world is not to be divided into sheep and goats. Not all things are black nor all things white. . . . Only the human mind invents categories and tries to force facts into separate pigeonholes. The living world is a continuum in each and every one of its aspects. The sooner we learn this concerning human sexual behavior the sooner we shall reach a sound understanding of the realities of sex."

"Sound understanding of the realities of sex" is not furthered by creating the myth of a new national disease of which 50 million people are victims. Nor is "sound understanding" increased by labeling disease as "health" in the name of an equally mythological "heterosexual-homosexual balance."

# McCarthy-Era Persecution of Homosexuals Provokes Resistance

LILLIAN FADERMAN

*Lillian Faderman has published numerous books and articles in the field of gay and lesbian history. Her book* Odd Girls and Twilight Lovers *chronicles the history of lesbian life in twentieth-century America. In this selection from her book, she documents the atmosphere of repression after World War II that intensified the persecution of gay and lesbian citizens. Hyperbolic propaganda about dangerous enemies—especially the Soviet Union and Communists in general—inspired a culture of fear in which those who broke from convention were stigmatized. Many Americans at this time supported a national agenda to purge the government of homosexual workers. While life was hard for gays and lesbians during this repressive era, the escalating persecution also inspired them to seek support in communities of their own making. Thoughts about resisting oppression began to emerge in the growing gay and lesbian subculture.*

The social upheaval occasioned by [World War II] was more than many Americans could bear. The years after became an age of authority, in the hope that authority would set the country back in balance. The pronouncements of those in charge, not only in the medical profession but in government as well, were virtually sacrosanct. There was little challenge to their notion that "extreme threats," such as the encroachments of the Soviets, required extreme solutions to weed out those who did not accept the reigning views. A breaking point in American rationality, justice, and common decency ensued. If political conformity was essential to national security, sexual conformity came to be considered, by some mystifying twist of logic by those in authority, as no less essential. In a decade of reaction, while women were sent back to the home, dissidents of every kind were deprived of their livelihoods and even packed off to jail.

## Targets of Persecution

Twentieth-century American witch-hunts began not long after the war. Those accused of Communism were their first target, but persecution quickly spread to other unpopular groups. Despite figures that [scientist] Alfred Kinsey gathered during these years, which showed that 50 percent of American men and 28 percent of American women had what could be considered "homosexual tendencies" (that is, homo-erotic interest in the same sex at some point in their adult lives), the statistical normality of same-sex love was now denied more fiercely than ever. The "homosexual" became a particular target of persecution in America. He or she presented an uncomfortable challenge to the mood that longed for obedience to an illusion of uncomplicated "morality." Even Kinsey was suspected of being a subversive, merely because he said that so many people in his studies admitted to same-sex attractions and experiences. Dr. Edmund Bergler angrily wrote in the *Psychiatric Quarterly* about Kinsey's statistics on widespread homosexuality in America that Kinsey had created a "myth of a new national disease." That "myth" would be "politically and propagandistically used against the United States abroad, stigmatizing the nation as a whole in a whisper campaign." Homosexuality was a detriment to the country's image and standing in the world. As far as those who spoke for mid-twentieth-century heterosexual America were concerned, homosexuality was a love that had better not dare speak its name. The heterosexual majority tyrannized. As one writer expressed it in 1951, if homosexuality was condemned by most people in a society, then loyalty to the society demanded that good citizens support condemnation of homosexuality and the laws against it.

By commonly accepted (though statistically erroneous) definition, the demarcation that separated "homosexual" from "heterosexual" was now more clear than ever. Between 1947 and 1950, 4,954 men and women were dismissed from the armed forces and civilian agencies for being homosexual. In 1950, the persecution escalated. Sen. Joseph McCarthy, whose barbarous tactics set the mood of the era, began by attracting attention as a Communist witch-hunter but soon saw an opportunity to broaden his field. Ironically, McCarthy's two aides were flamingly homosexual, even flitting about Europe as an "item [couple]," but that did not stop him from charging the State Department with knowingly harboring homosexuals and thereby placing the nation's security at risk.

## A Danger to American Integrity

The Republicans decided to make political hay out of the issue. Republican National Chairman Guy George Gabrielson wrote in the official party newsletter early in 1950 that "perhaps as dangerous as the actual communists are the sexual perverts who have infiltrated our government in recent years." By April of that year ninety-one homosexuals were fired from the State Department alone. In May 1950, New York Republican Governor [Thomas] Dewey accused President Truman and the Democrats of tolerating not only spies and traitors in government service, but also sexual perverts. Soon after, the Senate Appropriations Subcommittee joined the attacks, recommending that homosexuals be dismissed from government jobs since they were poor security risks because of their vulnerability to blackmail. Just as the number of women who dared to live as lesbians was increasing during the postwar years, their persecution was increasing as well—not just because of personal prejudices against them, but as a result of national policy.

Despite the general pretense, the concern about homosexuals in government was not primarily that they constituted a security risk because they were vulnerable to blackmail: that could have been obviated if the government simply declared that no one was to be fired on the ground of homosexuality. The concern was actually caused by discomfort with whatever was different. In fact, the Senate subcommittee admitted that there were two reasons why homosexuals should not be employed in government; that homosexuals were a security risk was only the second reason. The first was that "they are generally unsuitable," which was explained to mean that homosexuality "is so contrary to the normal accepted standards of social behavior that persons who engage in such activity are looked upon as outcasts by society in general." Official policy therefore became to persecute "outcasts." That the matter of security risk was only of secondary interest is demonstrated through the committee's recommendation that homosexuals be dismissed not only from the State Department, the military, and Congress, but also from occupations such as caretaker at the Botanical Gardens.

One woman who was affected by the Senate Subcommittee recommendation recalls that she was fired in 1951 from a job that had absolutely nothing to do with "national security." She had been doing social relief work in Germany for a private agency. Like all organizations operating in occupied territory, the agency had to be approved by the State Department and was subject to all its regulations. Through a "security check" of her past, it was discovered that not only had this woman gone to a psychotherapist in the

1940s, but she had discussed lesbianism with him. Though she had had no lesbian experiences since she took the job in Germany and was even trying to live a heterosexual life, she was nevertheless found undesirable because of her "homosexual tendencies." She had no recourse against her accusers. As she later observed of U.S. government tactics, "to be accused is to be guilty."

The Senate also justified the government policy of harassment of homosexuals by claiming that they must be fired from government jobs because of the "lack of emotional stability which is found in most sex perverts and the weakness of their moral fiber." The cross-fertilization of ideas between government and the medical establishment was apparent. Both were bent on sexual conformity, and neither accepted any responsibility for establishing the truth of their allegations against homosexuals. Homosexuals were condemned by the most obvious of begged questions: they were by definition perverts, which meant that they were emotionally unstable and their moral fiber was weak.

While homosexual men bore the brunt of sexual witch-hunting by the government, women who loved women and who dared to live lesbian lifestyles became more than incidental victims. Although statistically they lost fewer jobs than their male counterparts since there were fewer women than men employed by the government, lesbians realized that for the public "homosexual" was a scare-term: it was horrifying whether it referred to men or women. Lesbians believed, with plenty of justification, that whatever opprobrium was expressed for gay males would apply to them also and their livelihood and community standing would be just as endangered if their secret were known.

## Purging the "Perverts"

By 1951, federal agencies were using lie detectors in loyalty investigations of men and women in supposedly "sensitive" government jobs to determine whether they were either Communists or homosexuals. It was clearly the intent of the

Senate, whose recommendations justified such measures, to include lesbians among those that were to be dismissed from government jobs, since the report on which the recommendation was based pointedly specified that 4 percent of the female population in the United States was lesbian. Republican floor leader of the Senate Kenneth Wherry, who was the co-author of that report, declared that he was on a "crusade to harry every last pervert from the Federal Government services." Under the influence of such thinking, the head of the Washington, D.C., Vice Squad requested increased appropriations, not only to hunt down male homosexuals but also to establish a "lesbian squad" to "rout out the females." Senator Wherry explained, with some confusion, the rationale for such actions to the *New York Post*:

> You can't hardly separate homosexuals from subversives. . . . Mind you, I don't say every homosexual is a subversive, and I don't say every subversive is a homosexual. But [people] of low morality are a menace in the government, whatever [they are], and they are all tied up together.

Such convictions about the connections between leftists and homosexuals were apparent in the nature of the interrogation that women who were under suspicion were forced to undergo. M.K., who held a high ranking civil service job in Albany, New York, tells of having been summoned to New York City by the U. S. Civil Service Commission in 1954 and being put through a four day ordeal. For the first three days she was confronted with "evidence" of her communist leanings, such as having danced with a (male) U.S.S.R. liaison officer in Seoul, Korea, when she served there a few years earlier, and having applied to visit a North Korean university. On the fourth day she was asked directly, "Are you a homosexual?" After her denial, she was informed that the government had unearthed evidence that she had lived with several women in the past and had gone overseas with one. With no better proof against her she was barred from federal government employment "for security reasons, on the grounds of moral turpitude."

## Suspicion and Stigma

The Senate Subcommittee report led finally to an Executive Order signed by President [Dwight] Eisenhower as one of his first acts in office. That Order mandated the investigation for homosexuality not only of persons in "sensitive" positions, but of any government employee and of all new applicants for positions. It permitted no judicial review. An employee who felt she was dismissed unfairly would have no recourse beyond her department. She could be fired merely on the basis of anonymous accusations. Homosexuals in state and local government jobs were harassed as well. Lesbians were particularly affected. Since so few women could become doctors or lawyers or business leaders during the 1950s, because professional schools by now generally discouraged females, middle-class lesbians were forced into those professions that were more available to them as women. They made careers in teaching and social work—government jobs in which, by virtue of sexual orientation, a lesbian broke the law every day she came to work, regardless of how good an employee she was.

## Abandoned by Potential Allies

Psychoanalysts and the government had done such a thorough job in promoting the irrational fear of homosexuality that even groups that should have seen themselves as allies because they were persecuted in the same way, and should have wanted to form a coalition to fight injustice, denounced homosexuals. Instead of banding together with homosexuals—as reactionaries accused them of doing— leftists were almost as bad in their homophobia as the government. Black lesbian poet Audre Lorde says that when in 1953 she worked on a committee to free Julius and Ethel Rosenberg she realized that the one taboo among those socially liberated people remained homosexuality:

I could imagine these comrades, Black and white, among whom color and racial differences could be openly examined and talked about, nonetheless one day asking me accusingly, "Are you or have you ever been a member of a homosexual relationship?"

To leftists, homosexuality was reason for suspicion and shunning not only because they deemed it—through myth and prejudice equaled only by the right—"bourgeois and reactionary," but also because it made an individual more susceptible to the FBI.

Not even the bravest bastion of liberalism, the American Civil Liberties Union, dared to offer a strong defense on the lesbian's behalf during those years. As astonishing as it may be in retrospect, the ACLU National Board of Directors affirmed in January 1957 that "homosexuality is a valid consideration in evaluating the security risk factor in sensitive positions" and made clear that unless it was an issue of entrapment or denial of due process, the ACLU was not going to fight battles on the side of homosexuals: "It is not within the province of the Union to evaluate the social validity of the laws aimed at the suppression or elimination of homosexuals," the Union declared. Although it took a liberal stand on all other issues, it literally advised lesbians that the best thing they could do would be to "abandon" their lesbianism and become heterosexual.

Although Sen. Joseph McCarthy was censured by the Senate in 1954 for his overly zealous witch-hunting, the spirit he helped establish lived on through that decade and into the next. Homosexuals in all walks of life, not just those who worked for the government, were hunted down. Not even young college students were safe. In 1955 the dean and assistant dean of students at [the University of California–Los Angeles] published an article in the journal *School and Society* lamenting the "attraction of colleges, both public and private, for overt, hardened homosexuals" and recommending that all "sexually deviate" students be routed out of colleges if they were unwilling to undergo psychiatric treatment to change their sexual orientation. Students entering state supported universities were obliged to take a battery of tests in which thinly veiled questions on sexual preference appeared over and over. What the authorities expected such tests to reveal is unimaginable, since homosexuals who were smart enough to get into those institutions were surely smart enough to realize that they must dissemble. The 1950s mandated that women learn to lead a double existence if they wanted to live as lesbians and yet maintain the advantages of middle-class American life such as pursuing higher education and the careers to which it led. As one midwestern woman recalls, "If anyone ever asked if you were a lesbian you knew that you needed to deny it to your dying breath." They understood that if they could not develop the skill of hiding, if they were not wily enough to answer "no" to any form of the question "Are you or have you ever been . . . ," they would not survive as social beings.

## In the News

The popular press saw nothing objectionable in the ubiquitous harassment of homosexuals. In fact, stories of lesbian conspiracies and the dangers posed by those who were sexually "abnormal" were treated with great relish. In their scandalous *Washington Confidential*, for example, Jack Lait and Lee Mortimer announced that psychologists and sociologists who had "made a study of the problem" in the D.C. area believed "there are at least twice as many Sapphic lovers as fairies" and reeled off the names of several bars where lesbians sported with homosexual men, observing "all queers are in rapport with all other queers."

Mass circulation magazines presented homosexuality as a chief cause of American ills in articles with titles such as "New Moral Menace to Our Youth," in which same-sex love was said to lead to "drug addiction, burglary, sadism, and even murder." Lesbians were presented in those magazines as "preying" on innocent "victims." As *Jet*, a black magazine, characterized the lesbian in 1954, "If she so much as gets one foot into a good woman's home with the intention of seducing her, she will leave no stone unturned . . . and eventually destroy her life for good."

Such sensationalism was not limited to *National Enquirer*–type trash literature. For instance, *Human Events*, a weekly Washington newsletter that purported a readership of "40,000 business and professional leaders," declared, echoing the insanity of Senator Wherry, that homosexuals must be hunted down and purged because "by the very nature of their vice they belong to a sinister, mysterious, and efficient international [conspiracy, and] members of one conspiracy are prone to join another conspiracy."

If a magazine attempted to present homosexuality in a better light it was subject to censorship. In 1954 when the newly established homophile magazine *One* published a short story about a woman choosing to become a lesbian, "Sappho Remembered," the Postmaster General of Los Angeles confiscated all copies of the issue that had been mailed and demanded that the publisher prove that the story was not "obscene, lewd, lascivious and filthy." With blatantly homophobic reasoning, the federal district court upheld the Postmaster General's decision, arguing about "Sappho Remembered":

> This article is nothing more than cheap pornography calculated to promote lesbianism. It falls far short of dealing with homosexuality from a scientific, historic, or critical point of view. . . . An article may be vulgar, offensive and indecent even though not regarded as such by a particular group . . . because their own social or moral standards are far below those of the general community. . . . Social standards are fixed by and for the great majority and not by and for a hardened or weakened minority.

Obviously what the Court meant by "dealing with homosexuality from a scientific, historic, or critical point of view" was simply supporting the prevailing prejudice that homosexuality was diseased or sinful.

# Lesbian Novels

That pulp novels with lesbian subject matter should have been permitted to proliferate during this period is not as surprising as it may seem at first glance, since they were generally cautionary tales: "moral" literature that warned females that lesbianism was sick or evil and that if a woman dared to love another woman she would end up lonely and suicidal. On the surface, at least, they seemed to confirm social prejudices about homosexuality. But despite that, many lesbians read those novels avidly.

The pulps, with their lurid covers featuring two women exchanging erotic gazes or locked in an embrace, could be picked up at newsstands and corner drugstores, even in small towns, and they helped spread the word about lesbian lifestyles to women who might have been too sheltered otherwise to know that such things existed. Lesbians bought those books with relish because they learned to read between the lines and get whatever nurturance they needed from them. Where else could one find public images of women loving women? Of course the characters of the lesbian pulps almost always lived in shame and with the knowledge that, as the titles often suggested, they belonged in "twilight," "darkness," or "shadows." Self-hatred was requisite in these novels. Typically the lesbian was characterized by lines such as "A sword of self-revulsion, carefully shielded, slipped its scabbard now for one second to stab deeply to the exposed core of her lesbianism." But often the hooks suggested that lesbianism was so powerful that a heterosexual woman only had to be exposed to a dyke and she would fall (though she was usually rescued, rather perfunctorily, by a male before the last pages—in which the real lesbian was shown to be doomed to suitable torment). Lesbians could ignore their homophobic propaganda and moralizations and peruse the pulps for "their romance and charged eroticism."

Perhaps lesbians knew enough to be realistic about the limitations of the publishing industry. Just as they needed to be careful in their own lives, writers and publishers needed to be careful: novels with lesbian subject matter and even fairly explicit sexual scenes could escape censorship if they had "redeeming social value," which meant that they could not "legitimize the abnormal condition [of lesbianism]" by showing lesbians as anything other than ultimately defeated.

Writers who through their personal experiences might have been able to present more honest and happier depictions of lesbians did not dare to, even if they could have gotten such a book published. For example, novelist Helen Hull (*Quest, Labyrinth*), who spent much of her adult life in a love relationship with academic Mabel Robinson, was inspired by the Kinsey report in 1953 (that showed such a high incidence of lesbian experience in America) to think about writing a novel on lesbianism. She observed in her writer's journal that such a novel could show "what I have always thought, that conduct is not in any way consistent with either social code or law." Hull reflected that most of the women she knew best had not conformed to the stated mores of their society, "even when they have been important through their work and recognized positions." She briefly considered putting some of those lesbian friends into a novel: "K. . . . had courage and serenity, had groups of followers, must have had people whom she helped; E. had courage and liveliness and capacity for work and ingeniousness about developing her school. . . . She kept her sanguineness and her invincibility." But such people, who could have been much-needed role models for young women who chose to live as lesbians, never got into a lesbian novel because Hull concluded, as would most women writers with a reputation at stake during the period, that after all, "I don't want to be connected with the subject [of lesbianism]."

## In the Closet

It was not true, of course, that lesbians during the 1950s invariably paid for their nonconformity through misery, as the pulp novelists said they did. But whatever joy they found had to be procured outside of the main social institutions, and they had to be clandestine about it in a society that withheld from them the blessings it gave freely to all heterosexuals. Front marriages with gay men were not uncommon during the 1950s, not only for the sake of passing as heterosexual at work, but also in order to hide the truth from parents who could not bear their own failure in having raised a sexual non-conformist and who might have a daughter committed to a mental hospital for lesbianism. Lesbians often felt they could not trust close acquaintances with knowledge of their personal lives, even if they suspected those acquaintances might also be lesbian. A Vermont woman remembers, "Everyone was very cagey. We pretended to ourselves that we didn't talk about it because it shouldn't matter in a friendship, just as being a Democrat or a Republican shouldn't matter between friends. But the real reason we never talked about it was that if we weren't 100 percent sure the other person was gay too, it would be awful to be wrong. We'd be revealing ourselves to someone who probably couldn't understand and that could bring all sorts of trouble." It was a climate calculated to lead to paranoia, and many lesbians never overcame it, even when times improved.

It was also a climate that stripped lesbians of the possibility of self-defense by making it dangerous for them to organize effectively. The decade following the war that expanded the potential of lesbian lifestyles did see the formation of the first lesbian organization in America, Daughters of Bilitis (DOB), which was originally founded as a private social group to give middle-class lesbians an alternative to the gay bar scene. That such an organization could have been started in the 1950s is testimony to the war years' effectiveness in creating something of a self-conscious lesbian community. DOB was not interested for long in remaining a social club. It soon became involved in "improving the lesbian image" and demanding lesbian rights. But an organization that valiantly attempted to be political in a time when the idea of rights for sexual minorities was inconceivable was bound to remain minuscule for a long while. . . .

## A Mixed Legacy

Lesbians inherited a mixed legacy from the 1940s and '50s, when lesbianism came to mean, much more than it had earlier, not only a choice of sexual orientation, but a social orientation as well, though usually lived covertly. While the war and the migration afterward of masses of women, who often ended up in urban centers, meant that various lesbian subcultures could be established or expanded, these years were a most unfortunate time for such establishment and expansion. Suddenly there were large numbers of women who could become a part of a lesbian subculture, yet also suddenly there were more reasons than ever for the subculture to stay underground. The need to be covert became one of the chief manifestations of lesbian existence for an entire generation—until the 1970s and, for some women who do not trust recent changes to be permanent, until the present. The grand scale institutional insanity that characterized the Cold War also affected many lesbians profoundly by causing them to live in guilt, pain, self-hatred born of internalizing the hideous stereotypes of lesbianism, and justified suspicion as well as paranoia. The 1950s were perhaps the worst time in history for women to love women.

However, even the persecution of the 1950s aided in further establishing lesbian subcultures. It made many women feel they had to band together socially to survive, since heterosexuals could seldom be trusted. And while it made lesbianism a love that dared not speak its name very loudly, nevertheless it *gave* it a name over and over again that became known to many more thousands of American women. Were it not for the publicity that was inevitably attendant on persecution, some women, even by the 1950s, might not have realized that there were so many who shared their desires and aspirations, that various lesbian subcultures existed, that lesbianism could be a way of life. Fanatical homophobes who would have preferred a conspiracy of silence with regard to lesbianism were right in believing that silence would best serve their ends. Each time the silence was broken—even by the hateful images of homosexuality that characterized the 1950s—more women who preferred women learned labels for themselves, sought and often found others who shared those labels, and came to understand that they might probe beneath the denigrating images that society handed them to discover their own truths.

THE
HISTORY
OF
ISSUES

## CHAPTER 2

# Gay Rights
# Activism

*Chapter Preface*

It is commonly believed that the modern gay rights movement was ignited by the famous Stonewall rebellion in 1969. Patrons of a New York gay bar, the Stonewall Inn, resisted being herded into paddy wagons by local police, ultimately inspiring riots throughout Greenwich Village for two nights. While this confrontation was a pivotal moment for gays and lesbians, activists had been organizing for gay rights on a national level for over a decade before the Stonewall uprising.

These early organizations were some of the first to conceive of gays and lesbians as a distinct minority group. Rejecting the negative connotations attached to the word *homosexual*, they invented their own term to characterize their groups in order to promote a positive view of their communities. They called themselves "homophile" organizations to emphasize the emotional component of same-sex love and to de-emphasize the sexual aspect. Two of the most famous homophile organizations were the Mattachine Society and the Daughters of Bilitis.

Most homophile organizations eventually adopted a conservative strategy to achieve social change. They tended to avoid open confrontation with authorities unless absolutely necessary. More often they lobbied for social acceptability by arguing that gays and lesbians could live according to the norms and values of mainstream society.

By the late 1960s the assimilationist strategies of homophile organizations were losing the support of many gays and lesbians. With the rise of sexual liberation rhetoric, radical civil rights and antiwar demonstrations, and the countercultural youth movement, gays and lesbians came to favor more militant methods to achieve equal rights. As homophile organizations gradually disappeared, they were replaced by gay liberation organizations such as the Gay Liberation Front, the Radicalesbians, and the Gay Activists Alliance. The new organizations openly celebrated gay and lesbian culture and called for profound changes in mainstream society.

# Early Homophile Organizations Pioneer Gay Rights

ROBERT J. CORBER

*It is often assumed that the gay rights movement started in the late 1960s after the Stonewall riots, but recent research has shed light on small but committed groups who began to work toward acceptance of homosexuality as early as 1951. The Mattachine Society consisted primarily of gay male members, and the Daughters of Bilitis organized to address lesbian issues. In resistance to prevalent stereotypes about homosexuality, early activists coined the term* homophile *to describe their organizations in more positive language.*

*Author Robert J. Corber describes the tension between various homophile organizations in the following selection. He explains that there was disagreement between activists who wanted to build a strong homosexual subculture and those who focused on assimilating into mainstream society. By the 1960s many gay activists were experimenting with confrontational tactics such as picketing, demonstrations, and government lobbying. With the rise of a gay liberation movement in the late 1960s, homophile organizations eventually dissolved and were replaced by more militant organizations that advocated mass mobilization to demand civil rights and cultural liberation. Corber is the author of several articles and books about the history of homosexuality, including* Homosexuality in Cold War America: Resistance and the Crisis of Masculinity.

Robert J. Corber, "Homophile Movement," in *Gay Histories and Cultures: An Encyclopedia*. New York: Garland Publishing, Inc., 2000. Copyright © 2000 by George E. Haggerty. All rights reserved. Reproduced by permission of Routledge/Taylor & Francis Group LLC and the author.

The homophile movement constituted the first wave of organized political activity in the United States aimed at securing civil rights for homosexuals and lesbians. In the 1950s, homosexual rights activists eager to combat the stereotype of the sex-obsessed homosexual began using the term *homophile* as a euphemism. The suffix was meant to suggest that homosexuality was an emotional as well as a sexual attraction and that homosexuals did not differ significantly from heterosexuals. The term was officially adopted by the movement in the early 1960s.

## Key Leaders

The early homophile movement was deeply influenced by the Communist Party's nationalistic approach to the "Negro question." Although the party's policy on homosexuality mirrored that of the government during the Cold War—it expelled homosexuals on the grounds that they could be blackmailed by its enemies—it provided homosexual rights activists with a powerful model. Henry Hay, Chuck Rowland, and Bob Hull, who in 1951 founded the Mattachine Society, the first homophile organization, were members of the Communist Party, relying heavily on the knowledge and organizing skills they had acquired as party activists. They formed discussion groups that sought to empower homosexuals by teaching them to see themselves as an oppressed minority with their own distinct culture. Membership remained small until, adopting a party strategy, the society organized a demonstration protesting police entrapment, an oppressive practice directly affecting the mass of gay men.

Another influential figure in the early homophile movement was Edward Sagarin, who wrote under the pseudonym Donald Webster Cory. His pioneering study of the similarities between gays and other oppressed minorities, *The Homosexual in America* (1950), provided homosexual rights activists with a less militant approach. Unlike Hay, Rowland, and Hull, he did not see the value of building a separate homosexual culture in which gays and lesbians could take pride. Deeply influenced by Gunnar Myrdal's landmark study of racism, *The American Dilemma* (1944), he argued that the homosexual's problems stemmed from societal disapproval and that education and policy reform would improve his situation. In his view, the practices and forms of identity (frequenting gay bars, cruising in public places, and so on) homosexuals had created in response to their oppression were pathological and should be repudiated. Like Myrdal, Sagarin believed deeply in the myth of the American melting pot, and he was convinced that if homosexuals simply demonstrated that they did not differ significantly from heterosexuals, then like other minoritized groups, they would eventually gain acceptance by mainstream Americans.

Sagarin's influence on the homophile movement was ultimately greater than that of the more radical founders of the Mattachine Society. In the context of the McCarthy witch-hunts, Hay, Rowland, and Hull's links to the Communist Party were a liability that made the movement doubly vulnerable to political repression. Although the three activists had broken with the party because of its policy on homosexuals, questions about their politics persisted, leading some members of the Mattachine Society to propose requiring a loyalty oath. Their party affiliation aside, the three's emphasis on the importance of building a homosexual culture may have asked too much of rank-and-file activists. Men and women constantly made aware of their differences from mainstream American society were understandably reluctant to risk further marginalization by embracing those differences. Sagarin, by contrast, offered a way of achieving equality that accentuated the similarities rather than the differences between homosexuals and heterosexuals. With the ascendance of his approach, the homophile movement shifted its priorities and goals, focusing on educating a hostile public rather than engaging in militant political action.

## An Element of Militancy

Although leaders withheld information about the movement's radical origins, Hay, Rowland, and Hull's political vision (their emphasis on the distinctiveness of homosexual culture, their goal of building a mass movement, their political militancy) remained a vital, if marginalized, force in the movement. Whereas Hay and Hull distanced themselves from the movement following the repudiation of their ideas by the Mattachine Society, Rowland became a writer for *One*, the most widely circulated of the magazines associated with the movement. Frustrated by the movement's political timidity, he advocated the use of more confrontational tactics. Even after he left the magazine in 1955, *One* continued to publish articles expressing a variety of viewpoints intended to spark controversy. Editorials regularly attacked the medical model of homosexuality. A monthly column reported on oppressive police practices such as bar raids and shakedowns. And writers debated whether the homosexual subculture was a source of strength and courage or a destructive force that instilled shame and self-hatred. In refusing to adopt a party line, *One* may have been more effective than official movement organizations in shaping the consciousness of average gays and lesbians.

## Toward Gay Liberation

In the 1960s, a new generation of activists, deeply influenced by the civil rights movement, proved more receptive to Hay, Rowland, and Hull's vision of a militant mass movement. In opposition to their leaders, these activists began to experiment with more confrontational tactics designed to attract the attention of the media. They picketed government agencies that expelled homosexuals and lesbians, lobbied for legislation barring discrimination, and organized demonstrations against police harassment. More interested in gaining the support of gays and lesbians than that of heterosexuals, they also tried to build a national organization of homophile groups modeled on the civil rights movement. But they were unable to overcome the ideological differences and organizational rivalries that had long divided the movement. The Daughters of Bilitis, an organization of lesbians founded in 1956, understandably resented the focus on issues such as sodomy laws that primarily affected gay men and discouraged its members from participating in the coalition. Other groups continued to believe in the efficacy of education and resented the new militancy. Although at a conference in 1968 the movement officially adopted the confrontational motto "Gay Is Good," the show of unity was largely symbolic. The disaffection of organizations such as the Daughters of Bilitis indicated that differences over strategy were greater than the radicals realized. Following the Stonewall rebellion of 1969, the movement collapsed, displaced by gay liberation.

# Gays Must Organize Against Oppression

HARRY HAY

*After reading Alfred Kinsey's groundbreaking 1948 book* Sexual Behavior in the Human Male, *Harry Hay was inspired to write a proposal for a new organization to support homosexuals and fight for their civil rights. Ever since his early teens when he discovered he was gay, Hay had dreamed of such an organization to counter the persecution and isolation that so many homosexuals experienced in the first half of the twentieth century. Kinsey's research about the prevalence of male homosexuality encouraged Hay to argue that homosexuals are an oppressed minority group, just like African Americans, Jews, and working-class laborers.*

*In the following selection, originally written in 1948 and revised in 1950, Hay outlines justifications for a gay organization he calls the International Bachelor's Fraternal Order for Peace and Social Dignity. Due to the extensive persecution of homosexuals in the 1940s and 1950s, Hay used the code words "bachelors" and "the Androgynous Minority" instead of "homosexuals" to avoid being harassed or arrested by the police. While it may seem common sense today to say that gays and lesbians are a sexual minority group, the average American did not conceive of gays as a minority before Hay articulated the idea. Many argue that this idea, along with his relentless determination to politically organize homosexuals, gave birth to the modern gay rights movement. Hay eventually convinced a small group of men in Los Angeles to meet in 1950 to develop the first gay rights organization in the United States, the Mattachine Society. In just a few years the society grew into a thriving organization with branches in dozens of American cities.*

A. Statement of aims and purposes [of the International Bachelor's Fraternal Order for Peace and Social Dignity].

1. With full realization that encroaching American Fascism, like unto previous impacts of International Fascism, seeks to bend unorganized and unpopular minorities into isolated fragments of social and emotional instability;

   With full realization that the socially censured Androgynous Minority was suborned, blackmailed, cozened, and stampeded into serving as hoodlums, stool pigeons, volunteer informers, concentration camp trustees, torturers, and hangmen, before it, as a minority, was ruthlessly exterminated;

   With full realization that the full significance of the government indictment against Androgynous Civil Servants, veiled under the sentiment that they "by the peculiar circumstances of their private lives lay themselves wide open to social blackmail by a Foreign Power," lies in the legal establishment of a second type of *guilt by association*;

   With the full realization that a *guilt by association* charge requires that the victim prove himself innocent against undisclosed charges (and is, therefore, impossible), and that a *guilt by association* charge can be leveled on the evidence of anonymous and malicious informers (and, therefore, cannot be fought), and that under the Government's announced plans for eventual 100% war production mobilization all commerce and production would be conducted under government contract—thus making it impossible for Androgynes to secure employment;

And with the full realization that Guilt of Androgyny *by association*, equally with Guilt of Communist sympathy *by association*, can be employed as a threat against any and every man and woman in our country as a whip to ensure thought control and political regimentation;

With the full realization that, in order to earn for ourselves any place in the sun, we must with perseverance and self-discipline work collectively on the side of peace, for the program of the four freedoms of the Atlantic Charter, and in the spirit and letter of the United Nations Charter, for the full first-class citizenship participation of Minorities everywhere, including ourselves;

We, the Androgynes of the world, have formed this responsible corporate body to demonstrate by our efforts that our physiological and psychological handicaps need be no deterrent in integrating 10% of the world's population towards the constructive social progress of mankind.

2. We declare our aims to be to effect socially, economically, politically, and morally, the integration of the best interests of the Androgynous minority with the common good of the community in which we live.

3. We declare our aims to present the concept of our Fraternal Orders, fully subscribed to by our membership, as being similar in both membership service and community service and social objectives as the well-known and respected "Alcoholics Anonymous."

4. We aim, by helping our members to adjust emotionally and intellectually to the enlightened mores and ethics of the standard community, to eradicate the vicious myths and taboos that physiological deviation (degeneracy in its true scientific sense) precludes psychological and social degeneracy. (Within

the recognized minorities, people are bad not because they are Jews or Negroes but because of the external nature of their political and economic environments. We must endeavor to understand ourselves and then demonstrate this knowledge to the community.)

5. We aim to aid in the dispelling of this myth by attempting to regulate the social conduct of our minority in such matters as, for example, exhibitionism, indiscriminate profligacy, violations of public decency; we aim to explore and promote a socially healthy approach to the ethical values of a constructed pairing between Androgynes; we aim to tackle the question of profligacy and Satyriasis as emotional diseases to be treated clinically.

6. We aim to dispel the fears and antagonisms of the community by making available clinical personnel, specialists, and apparati to educators, churchmen, and professional practitioners to the end of discovering and applying group or personal techniques of therapy and/or guidance, to give advice or recommendations or assistance to outside community bodies perplexed by manifestations of an Androgynous nature or character; we aim by the above equipment to help curb the malingering and the inducements professed to be common to cases of juvenile delinquents; we aim by the above equipment to help community organizations adjust and alleviate where possible the emotional and psychological development of Androgynous tendencies in minors.

7. We aim, by making available to biologists, physiochemists, psychologists, and educators, clinical experience and data on the objectives, frustrations, daily patterns, oppressions, insecurities, compromises, and fruitions of the great body of average Androgynes, to represent to the community a codified social analysis upon which constructive and pro-

gressive sexual legislation may be comprehended and enacted.

8. We aim to contribute to the general welfare of the community by making common cause with other minorities in contributing to the reform of judicial, police, and penal practices which undermine the honesty and morale of the community.

9. We aim to contribute to the general morale of the community by bringing ourselves to realize that only in a national community embodying the right to freedom of conscience, the right to the expression of personal opinion, and the objective of a peaceful and mutually cooperative world affording equal place to cultural production as to industrial production can our minority realize and contribute its full value.

10. We aim to integrate ourselves into the constructive social progress of society, on the side of peace, for the program of the four freedoms of the Atlantic Charter, and in the spirit and letter of the United Nations Charter, by providing a collective outlet for political, cultural, and social expression to some 10% of the world's population, in which the collective force of their vote and voice may have substance and value.

B. Activities.

1. A Service Organization providing:

   a. Committee channels to work for positive, scientifically predicated, and morale building legislation.

   b. Committee channels to fight against, and eliminate, police brutality, political and judicial shakedown, and civic blackmail.

   c. Committee channels to educate public opinion.

   d. Committee channels to supplement community campaigns for minority rights; for safeguarding and restoring Constitutional Democracy on every Level; for promoting and insuring International Peace and the self-determination of nations and national minorities.

e. Committee channels to make available to the community whatever apparatus we may develop which has valuable community application (see A-6, 7, 8; see also B-3 below).
2. A Civil Insurance Organization providing:
   a. Through dues payments and standard computed fees, legal services for all civil infractions, shakedowns, frame-ups, blackmail, slander, and unwarranted invasions of personal privacy, as applicable legally to Androgynous experience.
   b. Through standard fees, bail in all cases, preliminary to review by the Orders' Grievance Committee to determine if the action involves any of the protectable categories outlined in B-1 above.
      (1) If clause B-1 is invoked, the Orders' insurance is to cover all basic costs of the case.
      (2) If clause B-1 is *not* invoked, the Orders' insurance does not apply. (But the Orders' Service and Welfare Committees will endeavor to work and press for judicial and community leniency, and will offer to take such cases under guardianship and apply therapy or guidance under the jurisdiction and supervision of the Court.)
      (3) If clause B-1 is invoked, the Order will make every effort to safeguard the social and economic well-being of the member and will undertake rehabilitation if necessary.
3. A Welfare and Educational Organization providing:
   a. Educational Study groups and membership Forums on the issues which concern the civic responsibilities, general welfare campaigns, and constitutional requirements of the community as a whole, *in which the membership by its aims requires the right to participate.*
   b. Educational study groups and membership Forums on the special issues which the Order is sworn to promote and promulgate.

c. Cultural, creative, and recreational activities towards the end of improving the social conditions of culture, under the organizing impact of craftsman-and-audience constant participation.

d. Welfare groups to promote a better social integration of the membership Minority into the community-at-large:

(1) This shall include series of group discussions on ethics, hygiene, ethnology, social anthropology, social custom, morality, genetics, etc.

(2) This shall include therapeutic groups conducted in accordance with the most advanced available techniques.

(3) This shall include scholastic and laboratory research into the most advanced physiological and psychological theories, techniques, and applications, for the benefit of membership needs and aims, and the needs of the community as a whole.

(4) This shall include committees and flying squads of specialists and qualified personnel, available for individual membership needs and problems, available to community needs and problems, and available to judiciary and governmental consultations, paroles, suspensions, and guardianships.

e. First Aid squads and single volunteers on a 24-hour basis to provide therapy, guidance, or counsel to members in emotional and psychological distress.

f. Social Service Committee to help new members, and members new to this community, to adjust themselves to the duties, the responsibilities, and the privileges of the local Orders' Chapter.

g. Public Relations Committee composed of civic advisors, churchmen, attorneys, doctors, qualified members, and interested persons to suggest activities and services based on current community interests.

h. The above suggested activities may be carried on under close supervision on a cooperative or token fee basis as determined by the membership body of the Chapter.

C. Membership.

1. Membership shall be declared to be completely nondiscriminatory as to race, color, creed, or political affiliation and shall be limited only to those actively affirming the principles of majority democracy, practiced within the Order, as outlined in A-1 above.

2. Membership shall be anonymous to the community at large and to each other if they choose: membership shall be protected by the device of fictitious names until such times as the organization is in a position to incorporate and set into operation the Civil Insurance plan.

3. Membership and inter-Order activity shall be Masonic in character; shall be understood to be sworn to protective secrecy except inasmuch as certain aims, purposes, and committees shall be declared as parties to community action or campaign.

4. Membership shall be determined by member-recommendation only and shall be confirmed by election. Members shall enter an initiate period for one year before being confirmed and during this period the Civil Insurance Coverage shall apply only at the discretion of the Executive Board. (Mechanics to be further determined.)

5. Membership shall, at all times, require of members and initiate an established minimum of active and unsolicited participation in at least one Educational-Welfare activity and one Service activity of the Orders' Chapter.

6. Membership shall be classified into five degrees of

rank which shall be determined and bestowed by membership vote.

| | |
|---|---|
| a. Initiate Degree | Insignia . . . pin showing IBFO |
| b. First Degree (requirement: recognized participation in Service & Welfare activity) | Insignia . . . pin showing IBFO bar showing Androgyne (in Greek) |
| c. Second Degree (requirement: achievement in community integration activity) | Insignia . . . pin showing IBFO bar showing Berdache (in Hopi) |
| d. Third Degree (requirement: continual leadership in Orders' Aims and Purposes) | Insignia . . . pin showing IBFO bar design designating Order of St. Medardus |
| e. Fourth Degree (requirement: the highest honor bestowable) | Insignia . . . pin and bars as described before, plus escutcheon and chain showing the Egyptian Ankh ♀, the sign of the Order of Pharaoh, the historic personification of the Androgynous Ideal |

7. Membership shall agree to at all times, whether able to be involved or not, to lend a willing ear and voice to programs and purposes considered basic to the described objectives of the Orders.

8. Membership shall agree that at all times leadership principles and activity principles shall be weighed

and accepted in terms of their adherence to the objectives, in spirit and in letter, as described in section A-1 above. Membership shall agree that at any time it becomes apparent that membership activity and sentiment is not in accord with the objectives and principles described in A above, that the dissenting member is required to submit his resignation, that the dissenting chapter is considered suspended preliminary to dissolution by the Executive Board, or that the organization as a whole is required to dissolve its incorporation and any and all connections with or interest in the name and prestige of this organization.

9. Membership shall subscribe to a minimum program of mutual aid and assistance, particularly to members who are new to a group or to a community. Similarly to Shrine and Masonic practice, insignia worn at an unconventional angle may be used to designate distress or need—and must be acted upon by all other members as quickly as possible.

D. Details of Organization (tentative and as yet incomplete).

1. The Orders shall be incorporated under the laws, duties and proscriptions attached to such non-profit organizations. Its corporate charter and by-laws must incorporate very precisely the objective and limitations of Section A and be subject to the proscriptions indicated in Section C-8.

2. The Orders shall be conceived to sub-charter supplementary subsidiaries such as:
   a. International Spinsters Orders.
   b. International Friends and Well-Wishers Auxiliaries.
   c. etc.

3. The Orders shall seek the aid and support of Church and Professional and Civic Leaders. The Orders shall seek the aid, and in return shall subscribe to the support of governmental reform bodies in the community; the Orders shall seek the cooperation

and respect of all minority groups, physical and moral welfare groups, and any other groups, whose general aims and purposes—both nationally and internationally—subscribe to the objectives described in A above.

4. The Orders declare that, at all times, they publicly subscribe (though anonymously except through the public face of the Orders) to the aims, tenets, and objectives described in Section A. If any individual, group, Chapter, or Division deny or betray by intent or action any and/or several of these tenets at any time, the Orders reserve the rights to dissolve and expel the offending Chapters or members, and shall do everything in its power to make social restitution for the offenses (see C-8; D-11).

5. For purposes of mutual protection and supervision, all inter-order activities and meetings shall be declared as "closed" to membership only, except as they may be singly designated for community assistance services or campaigns by the Majority decision of the Membership involved, at each instance and each occasion.

6. Meetings and committees shall be designed for compactness and mobility . . . and shall be closely supervised to insure optimal subscription to the basic requirements of community behavior. Membership recreational activities, in the name of the organization, shall be planned and designed with the amenabilities and censures of the community in mind. (For example, play-party and square dancing will probably be always acceptable where social dancing might not.)

7. Groups shall be mainly geographical except in regard to recreational and welfare groups as outlined in B-3 above.

8. Membership Lists shall be planned with the Optimal Anonymity in mind; after full and protective incorporation has been executed membership lists in coded

fictions and all data shall be handled by a bonded officer appointed by a duly elective and supervising governing committee.

9. The Orders, for the time being, shall be self-supporting as to needed funds and fees, and shall seek the services of paid functionaries only when the scope of Organizational activity requires it.

10. Insignia, referred to in C-6, must be earned by the member, and shall be bestowed by elective vote only in respect to degree of participatory service upon the part of the candidate.

    a. Any member who shall, in the course of a year, not advance the degree of his standing must agree to a review of his privileges and responsibilities and must agree to attempt to reach common decision with the committee as to his future commitments.

    b. This shall be construed as one of a number of safeguards of the protective mantle required by the Orders against the infiltration of elements inimicable to the aims and principles of the Orders and its individual members.

11. In relation to the public responsibility assured by the Orders as indicated in D-4, and cross-references above, it must be understood that should investigation reveal that the violation were a first deviation, or an irrational or compulsive slip from the self-discipline sought and subscribed to by the Orders that the organization reserves the right to treat the member, or members, as penitents and to invoke the protection of therapeutic guardianship under the leniency of the community.

# The Stonewall Riots Accelerate the Gay Rights Movement

JOHN D'EMILIO

*In the following selection John D'Emilio chronicles the 1969 uprising that occurred when police raided the Stonewall Inn, a gay bar in New York City. The ensuing riots, which mark the first time that gays and lesbians joined together en masse to protest police harassment, have become a milestone in the history of gay rights. D'Emilio traces the emergence of a new movement after Stonewall that came to be known as "gay liberation," which promoted militant activism to achieve societal changes in favor of gays and lesbians. This movement was a significant departure from the homophile movement, in which gay activists employed far less radical means of effecting change. Gay liberation groups encouraged all gays and lesbians to come out in order to shed self-hatred and to challenge homophobia in society. Many more gays and lesbians committed themselves to gay liberation than ever before, enabling the movement to achieve important progress toward equality for gays and lesbians. D'Emilio is a professor of history and the director of the Gender and Women's Studies Program at the University of Illinois–Chicago. This selection is excerpted from his book* Sexual Politics, Sexual Communities: The Making of a Homosexual Minority in the United States, 1940–1970.

John D'Emilio, *Sexual Politics, Sexual Communities: The Making of a Homosexual Minority in the United States, 1940–1970*. Chicago: University of Chicago Press, 1998. Copyright © 1998 by The University of Chicago. All rights reserved. Reproduced by permission.

On Friday, June 27, 1969, shortly before midnight, two detectives from Manhattan's Sixth Precinct set off with a few other officers to raid the Stonewall Inn, a gay bar on Christopher Street in the heart of Greenwich Village. They must have expected it to be a routine raid. New York was in the midst of a mayoral campaign—always a bad time for the city's homosexuals—and John Lindsay, the incumbent who had recently lost his party's primary, had reason to agree to a police cleanup. Moreover, a few weeks earlier the Sixth Precinct had received a new commanding officer who marked his entry into the position by initiating a series of raids on gay bars. The Stonewall Inn was an especially inviting target. Operating without a liquor license, reputed to have ties with organized crime, and offering scantily clad go-go boys as entertainment, it brought an "unruly" element to Sheridan Square, a busy Village intersection. Patrons of the Stonewall tended to be young and nonwhite. Many were drag queens, and many came from the burgeoning ghetto of runaways living across town in the East Village.

## A Surprise for the Police

However, the customers at the Stonewall that night responded in any but the usual fashion. As the police released them one by one from inside the bar, a crowd accumulated on the street. Jeers and catcalls arose from the onlookers when a paddy wagon departed with the bartender, the Stonewall's bouncer, and three drag queens. A few minutes later, an officer attempted to steer the last of the patrons, a lesbian, through the bystanders to a nearby patrol car. "She put up a struggle," the *Village Voice* reported, "from car to door to car again." At that moment,

> the scene became explosive. Limp wrists were forgotten. Beer cans and bottles were heaved at the windows and a rain of coins descended on the cops. . . . Almost by signal the crowd erupted into cobblestone and bottle heaving. . . . From nowhere came an uprooted parking meter—used as a battering ram on the Stonewall door. I

heard several cries of "let's get some gas," but the blaze of flame which soon appeared in the window of the Stonewall was still a shock.

Reinforcements rescued the shaken officers from the torched bar, but their work had barely started. Rioting continued far into the night, with Puerto Rican transvestites and young street people leading charges against rows of uniformed police officers and then withdrawing to regroup in Village alleys and side streets.

## Gay Power!

By the following night, graffiti calling for "Gay Power" had appeared along Christopher Street. Knots of young gays—effeminate, according to most reports—gathered on corners, angry and restless. Someone heaved a sack of wet garbage through the window of a patrol car. On nearby Waverly Place, a concrete block landed on the hood of another police car that was quickly surrounded by dozens of men, pounding on its doors and dancing on its hood. Helmeted officers from the tactical patrol force arrived on the scene and dispersed with swinging clubs an impromptu chorus line of gay men in the middle of a full kick. At the intersection of Greenwich Avenue and Christopher Street, several dozen queens screaming "Save Our Sister!" rushed a group of officers who were clubbing a young man and dragged him to safety. For the next few hours, trash fires blazed, bottles and stones flew through the air, and cries of "Gay Power!" rang in the streets as the police, numbering over 400, did battle with a crowd estimated at more than 2,000.

After the second night of disturbances, the anger that had erupted into street fighting was channeled into intense discussion of what many had begun to memorialize as the first gay riot in history. [Poet] Allen Ginsberg's stature in the 1960s had risen almost to that guru for many counterculture youth. When he arrived at the Stonewall on Sunday evening, he commented on the change that had already taken place. "You know, the guys there were so beautiful," he told a reporter. "They've lost that wounded look that fags all had ten years ago." The New York Mattachine Society [a gay rights organization] hastily assembled a special riot edition of its newsletter that characterized the events, with camp humor, as "The Hairpin Drop Heard Round the World." It scarcely exaggerated. Before the end of July, women and men in New York had formed the Gay Liberation Front [GLF], a self-proclaimed revolutionary organization in the style of the New Left. Word of the Stonewall riot and GLF spread rapidly among the networks of young radicals scattered across the country, and within a year gay liberation groups had sprung into existence on college campuses and in cities around the nation.

## The Time for Liberation

The Stonewall riot was able to spark a nationwide grassroots "liberation" effort among gay men and women in large part because of the radical movements that had so inflamed much of American youth during the 1960s. Gay liberation used the demonstrations of the New Left as recruiting grounds and appropriated the tactics of confrontational politics for its own ends. The ideas that suffused youth protest found their way into gay liberation, where they were modified and adapted to describe the oppression of homosexuals and lesbians. The apocalyptic rhetoric and the sense of impending revolution that surrounded the Movement by the end of the decade gave to its newest participants an audacious daring that made the dangers of a public avowal of their sexuality seem insignificant.

In order to make their existence known, gay liberationists took advantage of the almost daily political events that young radicals were staging across the country. New York's Gay Liberation Front had a contingent at the antiwar march held in the city on October 15, 1969, and was present in even larger numbers at the November moratorium weekend in Washington, where almost half a million activists rallied against American involvement in Southeast Asia. Gay radicals in Berkeley performed guerrilla theater on the campus during orientation that fall and carried banners at the November antiwar rally in San Francisco. In November 1969 and again the following May, lesbians from GLF converged on the Congress to Unite Women, which brought to New York women's liberationists from around the East. Gay activists ran workshops at the 1969 annual convention of the National Student Association. In May 1970 a GLF member addressed the rally in New Haven in support of Bobby Seale and Ericka Huggins, the imprisoned Black Panther leaders. A large contingent of lesbians and gay men attended the national gathering called by the Panthers in the fall of 1970, and the next year a gay "tribe" took part in the May Day protests in Washington against the war. In raising the banner of gay liberation at these and other local demonstrations, radical gays reached closeted homosexuals and lesbians in the Movement who already had a commitment to militant confrontational politics. Their message traveled quickly through the networks of activists created by the New Left, thus allowing gay liberation to spread with amazing rapidity.

The first gay liberationists attracted so many other young radicals not only because of a common sexual identity but because they shared a similar political perspective. Gay liberationists spoke in the hyperbolic phrases of the New Left. They talked of liberation from oppression, resisting genocide, and making a revolution against "imperialist Amerika." GLF's statement of purpose, printed in the New Left newspaper *RAT*, sounded like many of the documents produced by radicals in the late 1960s, except that it was written by and about homosexuals:

> We are a revolutionary group of men and women formed with the realization that complete sexual liberation for all people cannot come about unless existing social institutions are abolished. We reject society's attempt to impose sexual roles and definitions of our nature. We are

stepping outside these roles and simplistic myths. We are going to be who we are. At the same time, we are creating new social forms and relations, that is, relations based upon brotherhood, cooperation, human love, and uninhibited sexuality. Babylon has forced us to commit ourselves to one thing—revolution!

Gay liberation groups saw themselves as one component of the decade's radicalism and regularly addressed the other issues that were mobilizing American youth. The Berkeley GLF, for instance, passed a resolution on the Vietnam War and the draft demanding that "all troops be brought home at once" and that homosexuals in the armed forces "be given Honorable discharges immediately." Its Los Angeles counterpart declared its "unity with and support for all oppressed minorities who fight for their freedom" and expressed its intention "to build a new, free and loving Gay counter-culture." Positions such as these made it relatively easy for previously closeted but already radicalized homosexuals and lesbians to join or form gay liberation organizations, and the new movement quickly won their allegiance.

Gay liberationists targeted the same institutions as homophile militants, but their disaffection from American society impelled them to use tactics that their predecessors would never have adopted. Bar raids and street arrests of gay men in New York City during August 1970 provoked a march by several thousand men and women from Times Square to Greenwich Village, where rioting broke out. Articles hostile to gays in the *Village Voice* and in *Harper's* led to the occupation of publishers' offices. In San Francisco a demonstration against the *Examiner* erupted into a bloody confrontation with the police. Chicago Gay Liberation invaded the 1970 convention of the American Medical Association, while its counterpart in San Francisco disrupted the annual meeting of the American Psychiatric Association. At a session there on homosexuality a young bearded gay man danced around the auditorium in a red dress, while other homosexuals and lesbians scattered in the audience shouted "Genocide!" and "Torture!" during the reading of a paper on aversion therapy. Politicians campaigning for office found themselves hounded by scruffy gay militants who at any moment might race across the stage where they were speaking or jump in front of a television camera to demand that they speak out against the oppression of homosexuals. The confrontational tactics and flamboyant behavior thrust gay liberationists into the public spotlight. Although their actions may have alienated some homosexuals and lesbians, they inspired many others to join the movement's ranks.

## The Importance of "Coming Out"

As a political force, the New Left went into eclipse soon after gay liberation appeared on the scene, but the movement of lesbians and gay men continued to thrive throughout the 1970s. Two features of gay liberation accounted for its ability to avoid the decline that most of the other mass movements of the 1960s experienced. One was the new definition that post-Stonewall activists gave to "coming out," which doubled both as ends and means for young gay radicals. The second was the emergence of a strong lesbian liberation movement.

From its beginning, gay liberation transformed the meaning of "coming out." Previously coming out had signified the private decision to accept one's homosexual desires and to acknowledge one's sexual identity to other gay men and women. Throughout the 1950s and 1960s, leaders of the homophile cause had in effect extended their coming out to the public sphere through their work in the movement. But only rarely did they counsel lesbians and homosexuals at large to follow their example, and when they did, homophile activists presented it as a selfless step taken for the benefit of others. Gay liberationists, on the other hand, recast coming out as a profoundly political act that could offer enormous personal benefits to an individual. The open avowal of one's sexual identity, whether at work, at school, at home, or before television cameras, symbolized the shedding of the self-hatred that gay men and women internalized, and consequently it promised an immediate improvement in one's life. To come out of the "closet" quintessentially expressed the fusion of the personal and the political that the radicalism of the late 1960s exalted.

Coming out also posed as the key strategy for building a movement. Its impact on an individual was often cathartic. The exhilaration and anger that surfaced when men and women stepped through the fear of discovery propelled them into political activity. Moreover, when lesbians and homosexuals came out, they crossed a critical dividing line. They relinquished their invisibility, made themselves vulnerable to attack, and acquired an investment in the success of the movement in a way that mere adherence to a political line could never accomplish. Visible lesbians and gay men also served as magnets that drew others to them. Furthermore, once out of the closet, they could not easily fade back in. Coming out provided gay liberation with an army of permanent enlistees.

## Lesbian Feminism

A second critical feature of the post-Stonewall era was the appearance of a strong lesbian liberation movement. Lesbians had always been a tiny fraction of the homophile movement. But the almost simultaneous birth of women's liberation and gay liberation propelled large numbers of them into radical sexual politics. Lesbians were active in both early gay liberation groups and feminist organizations. Frustrated and angered by the chauvinism they experienced in gay groups and the hostility they found in the women's movement, many lesbians opted to create their own separatist organizations. Groups such as Radicalesbians in New York, the Furies Collective in Washington, D.C., and Gay Women's Liberation in San Francisco carved out a distinctive lesbian-feminist politics. They too spoke in the radical phrases of the New Left, but with an accent on the special revolutionary role that lesbians filled because of their dual oppression as women and as homosexuals. Moreover, as other lesbians made their way into gay and women's groups, their encounters with the chauvinism of gay men and the hostility of heterosexual feminists provided lesbian liberation with ever more recruits.

Although gay liberation and women's liberation both contributed to the growth of a lesbian-feminist movement, the latter exerted a greater influence. The feminist movement offered the psychic space for many women to come to a self-definition as lesbian. Women's liberation was in its origins a separatist movement, with an ideology that defined men as the problem and with organizational forms from consciousness-raising groups to action-oriented collectives that placed a premium on female solidarity. As women explored their oppression together, it became easier to acknowledge their love for other women. The seeming contradiction between an ideology that focused criticism on men per se and the ties of heterosexual feminists to males often provoked a crisis of identity. Lesbian-feminists played upon this contradiction. "A lesbian is the rage of all women condensed to the point of explosion," wrote New York Radicalesbians in "The Woman-Identified Woman," one of the most influential essays of the sexual liberation movements:

> Lesbian is the word, the label, the condition that holds women in line. . . . Lesbian is a label invented by the man to throw at any woman who dares to be his equal, who dares to challenge his prerogatives, who dares to assert the primacy of her own needs. . . . As long as women's liberation tries to free women without facing the basic heterosexual structure that binds us in one-to-one relationships with our own oppressors, tremendous energies will continue to flow into trying to straighten up each particular relationship with a man. . . . It is the primacy of women relating to women, of women creating a new consciousness of and with each other which is at

the heart of women's liberation, and the basis for the cultural revolution.

Under these circumstances many heterosexual women reevaluated their sexuality and resolved the contradiction between politics and personal life by coming out as lesbians. Lesbian-feminist organizations were filled with women who came not from the urban subculture of lesbian bars but from the heterosexual world, with the women's liberation movement as a way station. As opponents of feminism were quick to charge, the women's movement was something of a "breeding ground" for lesbianism.

Besides the encouragement it provided for women to come out, women's liberation served lesbians—and gay men—in another way. The feminist movement continued to thrive during the 1970s. Its ideas permeated the country, its agenda worked itself into the political process, and it effected deep-seated changes in the lives of tens of millions of women and men. Feminism's attack upon traditional sex roles and the affirmation of a nonreproductive sexuality that was implicit in such demands as unrestricted access to abortion paved a smoother road for lesbians and homosexuals who were also challenging rigid male and female stereotypes and championing an eroticism that by its nature did not lead to procreation. Moreover, lesbians served as a bridge between the women's movement and gay liberation, at the very least guaranteeing that sectors of each remained amenable to the goals and perspectives of the other. Feminism helped to remove gay life and gay politics from the margins of American society.

## Leaving a Legacy

By any standard of measurement, post-Stonewall gay liberation dwarfed its homophile predecessor. In June 1970 between 5,000 and 10,000 men and women commemorated the first anniversary of the riot with a march from Greenwich Village to Central Park. By the second half of the decade, Gay Freedom Day events were occurring in dozens of cities, and total participation exceeded half a million individuals. The fifty homophile organizations that had existed in 1969 mushroomed into more than 800 only four years later; as the 1970s ended, the number reached into the thousands. In a relatively short time, gay liberation achieved the goal that had eluded homophile leaders for two decades—the active involvement of large numbers of homosexuals and lesbians in their own emancipation effort.

Numerical strength allowed the new breed of liberationists to compile a list of achievements that could only have elicited awe from homophile activists. In 1973 the American Psychiatric Association altered a position it had held for almost a century by removing homosexuality from its list of mental disorders. During the 1970s more than half the states repealed their sodomy laws, the Civil Service Commission eliminated its ban on the employment of lesbians and homosexuals, and several dozen municipalities passed antidiscrimination statutes. Politicians of national stature came out in favor of gay rights. Activists were invited to the White House to discuss their grievances, and in 1980 the Democratic party platform included a gay rights plank.

The stress gay liberation placed upon coming out also gave the movement leverage of another kind. Not only did men and women join groups that campaigned for equality from outside American institutions; they also came out within their professions, their communities, and other institutions to which they belonged. Gay Catholics, for instance, formed Dignity, and gay Episcopalians, Integrity. In some denominations gay men and women sought not only acceptance but also ordination as ministers. Military personnel announced their homosexuality and fought for the right to remain in the service. Lesbian and gay male academicians, school teachers, social workers, doctors, nurses, psychologists, and others created caucuses in their professions to sensitize their peers to the needs of the gay community and to combat discrimination. Openly gay journalists and television reporters brought an insider's perspective to their coverage of gay-related news. The visibility of lesbians and gay men in so many varied settings helped make homosexuality seem less of a strange, threatening phenomenon and more like an integral part of the social fabric.

## Consciousness Raising

Finally, the post-Stonewall era witnessed a significant shift in the self-definition of gay men and women. As pressure from gay liberationists made police harassment the exception rather than the rule in many American cities, the gay subculture flourished as never before. The relative freedom from danger, along with the emphasis the movement placed on gay pride, led not only to an expansion of the bar world but also to the creation of a range of "community" institutions. Gay men and lesbians formed their own churches, health clinics, counseling services, social centers, professional associations, and amateur sports leagues. Male and female entrepreneurs built record companies, publishing houses, travel agencies, and vacation resorts. Newspapers, magazines, literary journals, theater companies, and film collectives gave expression to a distinctive cultural experience. The subculture of homosexual men and women became less exclusively erotic. Gayness and lesbianism began to encompass an identity that for many included a wide array of private and public activities.

Stonewall thus marked a critical divide in the politics and consciousness of homosexuals and lesbians. A small, thinly spread reform effort suddenly grew into a large, grassroots movement for liberation. The quality of gay life in America was permanently altered as a furtive subculture moved aggressively into the open.

# A Manifesto for Gay Liberation

CARL WITTMAN

*The following selection was one of the principal documents that inspired the gay liberation movement in the late 1960s. Author Carl Wittman, who had been a leader in the radical Students for a Democratic Society (SDS) group in earlier years, wrote "A Gay Manifesto" in the spring of 1969. It was reprinted in many leftist newspapers, where gay readers encountered it for the first time. Giving voice to an emerging liberationist perspective in the gay community, he outlines many of the principles that gay activists adopted in the 1960s and 1970s, especially in urban centers like San Francisco and New York. Unlike the homophile organizations that emphasized achieving legal rights and mainstream acceptance, liberationists celebrated the gay subculture identity that separated them from heterosexual America. Like other counterculture groups at the time, they encouraged egalitarian relationships, sexual freedom, and militant activism.*

San Francisco is a refugee camp for homosexuals: We have fled here from every part of the nation, and like refugees elsewhere, we came not because it is so great here, but because it was so bad there. By the tens of thousands, we fled small towns where to be ourselves would endanger our jobs and any hope of a decent life; we have fled from blackmailing cops, from families who disowned or "tolerated" us; we have been drummed out of the armed

Carl Wittman, "A Gay Manifesto," April 1969.

services, thrown out of schools, fired from jobs, beaten by punks and policemen.

And we have formed a ghetto, out of self-protection. It is a ghetto rather than a free territory because it is still theirs. Straight cops patrol us, straight legislators govern us, straight employers keep us in line, straight money exploits us. We have pretended everything is OK, because we haven't been able to see how to change it—we've been afraid.

## A Liberation Movement

In the past year [1969] there has been an awakening of gay liberation ideas and energy. How it began we don't know; maybe we were inspired by black people and their freedom movement; we learned how to stop pretending from the hip revolution. Amerika in all its ugliness has surfaced with the war and our national leaders. And we are revulsed by the quality of our ghetto life.

Where once there was frustration, alienation, and cynicism, there are new characteristics among us. We are full of love for each other and are showing it; we are full of anger at what has been done to us. And as we recall all the self-censorship and repression for so many years, a reservoir of tears pours out of our eyes. And we are euphoric, high with the initial flourish of a movement.

We want to make ourselves clear: our first job is to free ourselves; that means clearing our heads of the garbage that's been poured into them. This article is an attempt at raising a number of issues, and presenting some ideas to replace the old ones. It is primarily for ourselves, a starting point of discussion. If straight people of good will find it useful in understanding what liberation is about, so much the better.

It should also be clear that these are the views of one person, and are determined not only by my homosexuality, but my being white, male, middle-class. It is my individual consciousness. Our group consciousness will evolve as we get ourselves together—we are only at the beginning.

# I. On Orientation

1. *What homosexuality is:* Nature leaves undefined the object of sexual desire. The gender of that object is imposed socially. Humans originally made homosexuality taboo because they needed every bit of energy to produce and raise children: survival of the species was a priority. With overpopulation and technological change, that taboo continued only to exploit us and enslave us.

As kids we refused to capitulate to demands that we ignore our feelings toward each other. Somewhere we found the strength to resist being indoctrinated, and we should count that among our assets. We have to realize that our loving each other is a good thing, not an unfortunate thing, and that we have a lot to teach straights about sex, love, strength, and resistance.

Homosexuality is *not* a lot of things. It is not a makeshift in the absence of the opposite sex; it is not hatred or rejection of the opposite sex; it is not genetic; it is not the result of broken homes except inasmuch as we could see the sham of American marriage. *Homosexuality is the capacity to love someone of the same sex.*

2. *Bisexuality:* Bisexuality is good; it is the capacity to love people of either sex. The reason so few of us are bisexual is because society made such a big stink about homosexuality that we got forced into seeing ourselves as either straight or non-straight. Also, many gays got turned off to the ways men are supposed to act with women and vice-versa, which is pretty fucked-up. Gays will begin to turn on to women when 1) it's something that we do because we want to, and not because we should, and 2) when women's liberation changes the nature of heterosexual relationships.

We continue to call ourselves homosexual, not bisexual, even if we do make it with the opposite sex also, because saying "Oh, I'm Bi" is a copout for a gay. We get told it's OK to sleep with guys as long as we sleep with women, too, and that's still putting homosexuality down. We'll be gay until everyone has forgotten that it's an issue. Then we'll begin to be complete.

3. *Heterosexuality:* Exclusive heterosexuality is f——ed up. It reflects a fear of people of the same sex, it's anti-homosexual, and it is fraught with frustration. Heterosexual sex is f——ed up, too; ask women's liberation about what straight guys are like in bed. Sex is aggression for the male chauvinist; sex is obligation for the traditional woman. And among the young, the modern, the hip, it's only a subtle version of the same. For us to become heterosexual in the sense that our straight brothers and sisters are is not a cure, it is a disease.

## II. On Women

1. *Lesbianism:* It's been a male-dominated society for too long, and that has warped both men and women. So gay women are going to see things differently from gay men; they are going to feel put down as women, too. Their liberation is tied up with both gay liberation and women's liberation.

This paper speaks from the gay male viewpoint. And although some of the ideas in it may be equally relevant to gay women, it would be arrogant to presume this to be a manifesto for lesbians.

We look forward to the emergence of a lesbian liberation voice. The existence of a lesbian caucus within the New York Gay Liberation Front has been very helpful in challenging male chauvinism among gay guys, and anti-gay feelings among women's liberation.

2. *Male chauvinism:* All men are infected with male chauvinism—we were brought up that way. It means we assume that women play subordinate roles and are less human than ourselves. (At an early gay liberation meeting one guy said, "Why don't we invite women's liberation—they can bring sandwiches and coffee.") It is no wonder that so few gay women have become active in our groups.

Male chauvinism, however, is not central to us. We can

junk it much more easily than straight men can. For we understand oppression. We have largely opted out of a system which oppresses women daily—our egos are not built on putting women down and having them build us up. Also, living in a mostly male world we have become used to playing different roles, doing our own shit-work. And finally, we have a common enemy: the big male chauvinists are also the big anti-gays.

But we need to purge male chauvinism, both in behavior and in thought among us. Chick equals nigger equals queer. Think it over.

3. *Women's liberation:* They are assuming their equality and dignity and in doing so are challenging the same things we are: the roles, the exploitation of minorities by capitalism, the arrogant smugness of straight white male middle-class Amerika. They are our sisters in the struggle.

Problems and differences will become clearer when we begin to work together. One major problem is our own male chauvinism. Another is uptightness and hostility to homosexuality that many women have—that is the straight in them. A third problem is differing views on sex: sex for them has meant oppression, while for us it has been a symbol of our freedom. We must come to know and understand each other's style, jargon and humor.

## III. On Roles

1. *Mimicry of straight society:* We are children of straight society. We still think straight: that is part of our oppression. One of the worst of straight concepts is inequality. Straight (also white, English, male, capitalist) thinking views things in terms of order and comparison. A is before B, B is after A; one is below two is below three; there is no room for equality. This idea gets extended to male/female, on top/on bottom, spouse/not spouse, heterosexual/homosexual, boss/worker, white/black, and rich/poor. Our social institutions cause and reflect this verbal hierarchy. This is Amerika.

We've lived in these institutions all our lives. Naturally

we mimic the roles. For too long we mimicked these roles to protect ourselves—a survival mechanism. Now we are becoming free enough to shed the roles which we've picked up from the institutions which have imprisoned us. *"Stop mimicking straights, stop censoring ourselves."*

2. *Marriage:* Marriage is a prime example of a straight institution fraught with role playing. Traditional marriage is a rotten, oppressive institution. Those of us who have been in heterosexual marriages too often have blamed our gayness on the breakup of the marriage. No. They broke up because marriage is a contract which smothers both people, denies needs, and places impossible demands on both people. And we had the strength, again, to refuse to capitulate to the roles which were demanded of us.

Gay people must stop gauging their self-respect by how well they mimic straight marriages. Gay marriages will have the same problems as straight ones except in burlesque. For the usual legitimacy and pressures which keep straight marriages together are absent, e.g. kids, what parents think, what neighbors say.

To accept that happiness comes through finding a groovy spouse and settling down, showing the world that "we're just the same as you" is avoiding the real issues, and is all expression of self-hatred.

3. *Alternatives to marriage:* People want to get married for lots of good reasons, although marriage won't often meet those needs or desires. We're all looking for security, a flow of love, and a feeling of belonging and being needed.

These needs can be met through a number of social relationships and living situations. Things we want to get away from are: 1) exclusiveness, propertied attitudes toward each other, a mutual pact against the rest of the world; 2) promise about the future, which we have no right to make and which prevent us from, or make us feel guilty about, growing; 3) inflexible roles, roles which do not reflect us at the moment but are inherited through mimicry and inability to define equalitarian relationships.

We have to define for ourselves a new pluralistic, role-free social structure for ourselves. It must contain both the freedom and physical space for people to live alone, live together for awhile, live together for a long time, either as couples or in larger numbers; and the ability to flow easily from one of these states to another as our needs change.

Liberation for gay people is defining for ourselves how and with whom we live, instead of measuring our relationship in comparison to straight ones, with straight values.

4. *Gay "stereotypes"*: The straights' image of the gay world is defined largely by those of us who have violated straight roles. There is a tendency among "homophile" groups to deplore gays who play visible roles—the queens and the nellies. As liberated gays, we must take a clear stand. 1) Gays who stand out have become our first martyrs. They came out and withstood disapproval before the rest of us did. 2) If they have suffered from being open, it is straight society whom we must indict, not the queen.

5. *Closet queens:* This phrase is becoming analogous to "Uncle Tom." To pretend to be straight sexually, or to pretend to be straight socially, is probably the most harmful pattern of behavior in the ghetto. The married guy who makes it on the side secretly; the guy who will go to bed once but who won't develop any gay relationships; the pretender at work or school who changes the gender of the friend he's talking about; the guy who'll [perform oral sex] in the bushes but who won't go to bed.

If we are liberated we are open with our sexuality. Closet queenery must end. *Come out.*

But in saying come out, we have to have our heads clear about a few things: 1) Closet queens are our brothers, and must be defended against attacks by straight people; 2) The fear of coming out is not paranoia; the stakes are high: loss of family ties, loss of job, loss of straight friends— these are all reminders that the oppression is not just in our heads. It's real. Each of us must make the steps toward openness at our own speed and on our own impulses. Being open is the foundation of freedom: it has to be built solidly; 3) "Closet queen" is a broad term covering a multitude of forms of defense, self-hatred, lack of strength, and habit. We are all closet queens in some ways, and all of us had to come out—very few of us were "flagrant" at the age of seven! We must afford our brothers and sisters the same patience we afforded ourselves. And while their closet queenery is part of our oppression, it's more a part of theirs. They alone can decide when and how.

## IV. On Oppression

It is important to catalog and understand the different facets of our oppression. There is no future in arguing about degrees of oppression. A lot of "movement" types come on with a line of shit about homosexuals not being oppressed as much as blacks or Vietnamese or workers or women. We don't happen to fit into their ideas of class or caste. Bull! When people feel oppressed, they act on that feeling. We feel oppressed. Talk about the priority of black liberation or ending imperialism over and above gay liberation is just anti-gay propaganda.

1. *Physical attacks:* We are attacked, beaten, castrated and left dead time and time again. There are half a dozen known unsolved slayings in San Francisco parks in the last few years. "Punks," often of minority groups who look around for someone under them socially, feel encouraged to beat up on "queens," and cops look the other way. That used to be called lynching.

Cops in most cities have harassed our meeting places: bars and baths and parks. They set up entrapment squads. A Berkeley brother was slain by a cop in April when he tried to split after finding out that the trick who was making advances to him was a cop. Cities set up "pervert" registration, which if nothing else scares our brothers deeper into the closet.

One of the most vicious slurs on us is the blame for prison "gang rapes." These rapes are invariably done by people who consider themselves straight. The victims of these rapes are us and straights who can't defend themselves. The press campaign to link prison rapes with homosexuality is an attempt to make straights fear and despise us, so they can oppress us more. It's typical of the f——ed-up straight mind to think that homosexual sex involves tying a guy down and f——ing him. That's aggression, not sex. If that's what sex is for a lot of straight people, that's a problem they have to solve, not us.

2. *Psychological warfare:* Right from the beginning we have been subjected to a barrage of straight propaganda. Since our parents don't know any homosexuals, we grow up thinking that we're alone and different and perverted. Our school friends identify "queer" with any non-conformist or bad behavior. Our elementary school teachers tell us not to talk to strangers or accept rides. Television, billboards and magazines put forth a false idealization of male/female relationships, and make us wish we were different, wish we were "in." In family living class we're taught how we're supposed to turn out. And all along the best we hear about homosexuality is that it's an unfortunate problem.

3. *Self-oppression:* As gay liberation grows, we will find our uptight brothers and sisters, particularly those who are making a buck off our ghetto, coming on strong to defend the status quo. This is self-oppression: "don't rock the boat"; "things in SF are OK"; "gay people just aren't together"; "I'm not oppressed." These lines are right out of the mouths of the straight establishment. A large part of our oppression would end if we would stop putting ourselves and our pride down.

4. *Institutional oppression:* Discrimination against gays is blatant, if we open our eyes. Homosexual relationships are illegal, and even if these laws are not regularly enforced, they encourage and enforce closet queenery. The bulk of the social work/psychiatric field looks upon homosexuality as a problem, and treats us as sick. Employers let it be known that our skills are acceptable only as long as our

sexuality is hidden. Big business and government are particularly notorious offenders.

The discrimination in the draft and armed services is a pillar of the general attitude toward gays. If we are willing to label ourselves publicly not only as homosexual but as sick, then we qualify for deferment; and if we're not "discreet" (dishonest) we get drummed out of the service. Hell, no, we won't go, of course not, but we can't let the army f—— over us this way, either. . . .

## VII. On Coalition

Right now the bulk of our work has to be among ourselves—self educating, fending off attacks, and building free territory. Thus basically we have to have a gay/straight vision of the world until the oppression of gays is ended.

But not every straight is our enemy. Many of us have mixed identities, and have ties with other liberation movements: women, blacks, other minority groups; we may also have taken on an identity which is vital to us: ecology, dope, ideology. And face it: we can't change Amerika alone.

Who do we look to for coalition?

1. *Women's liberation:* Summarizing earlier statements, 1) they are our closest ally; we must try hard to get together with them; 2) a lesbian caucus is probably the best way to attack gay guys' male chauvinism, and challenge the straightness of women's liberation; 3) as males we must be sensitive to their developing identities as women, and respect that; if we *know what our* freedom is about, *they* certainly know what's best for *them.*

2. *Black liberation:* This is tenuous right now because of the uptightness and supermasculinity of many black men (which is understandable). Despite that, we must support their movement, particularly when they are under attack from the establishment; we must show them that we mean business; and we must figure out who our common enemies are: police, city hall, capitalism.

3. *Chicanos:* Basically the same problem as with blacks:

trying to overcome mutual animosity and fear, and finding ways to support them. The extra problem of super uptightness and machismo among Latin cultures, and the traditional pattern of Mexicans beating up "queers," can be overcome: we're both oppressed, and by the same people at the top.

4. *White radicals and ideologues:* We're not, as a group, Marxist or Communist. We haven't figured out what kind of political/economic system is good for us as gays. Neither capitalist or socialist countries have treated us as anything other than *non grata* [unacceptable] so far.

But we know we are radical, in that we know the system that we're under now is a direct source of oppression, and it's not a question of getting our share of the pie. The pie is rotten.

We can look forward to coalition and mutual support with radical groups if they are able to transcend their antigay and male chauvinist patterns. We support radical and militant demands when they arise, *e.g.* Moratorium, People's Park,[1] but only as a group; we can't compromise or soft-peddle our gay identity.

Problems: because radicals are doing somebody else's thing, they tend to avoid issues which affect them directly, and see us as jeopardizing their "work" with other groups (workers, blacks). Some years ago a dignitary of SDS [Students for a Democratic Society] on a community organization project announced at an initial staff meeting that there would be no homosexuality (or dope) on the project. And recently in New York, a movement group which had a coffee-house get-together after a political rally told the gays to leave when they started dancing together. (It's interest-

1. During the Vietnam Moratorium protests in 1969, an estimated 2 million people across the United States organized demonstrations against the Vietnam War. In April of that same year, a group of people took over a vacant patch of land on the University of California–Berkeley, campus to build People's Park, a gathering place for local residents. Three months later, when the university enlisted one hundred Highway Patrol officers to chase residents off the land, a violent conflict ensued among students, neighbors, and the National Guard.

ing to note that in this case, the only two groups which supported us were women's liberation and the Crazies.[2])

Perhaps most fruitful would be to broach with radicals their stifled homosexuality and the issues which arise from challenging sexual roles.

5. *Hip and street people:* A major dynamic of rising gay liberation sentiment is the hip revolution within the gay community. Emphasis on love, dropping out, being honest, expressing yourself through hair and clothes, and smoking dope are all attributes of this. The gays who are the least vulnerable to attack by the establishment have been the freest to express themselves on gay liberation.

We can make a direct appeal to young people, who are not so uptight about homosexuality. One kid, after having his first sex with a male, said, "I don't know what all the fuss is about; making it with a girl just isn't that different."

The hip/street culture has led people into a lot of freeing activities: encounter/sensitivity, the quest for reality, freeing territory for the people, ecological consciousness, communes. These are real points of agreement and probably will make it easier for them to get their heads straight about homosexuality, too.

*Homophile groups:* 1) Reformist or pokey as they sometimes are, they are our brothers. They'll grow as we have grown and grow. Do not attack them in straight or mixed company. 2) Ignore their attack on us. 3) Cooperate where cooperation is possible without essential compromise of our identity.

## Conclusion: An Outline of Imperatives for Gay Liberation

1. Free ourselves: come out everywhere; initiate self defense and political activity; initiate counter community institutions.

2. The Crazies were a small, anarchist liberation group active at the time Wittman wrote this selection.

2. Turn other gay people on: talk all the time; understand, forgive, accept.

3. Free the homosexual in everyone: we'll be getting a good bit of shit from threatened latents: be gentle, and keep talking and acting free.

4. We've been playing an act for a long time, so we're consummate actors. Now we can begin to be, and it'll be a good show!

# Gays Must Come Out and Fight for Their Rights

HARVEY MILK

*In 1978 Harvey Milk was elected to the San Francisco Board of Supervisors, becoming the first openly gay elected official in the city's history. His efforts to advance gay rights garnered national attention, and he became an important leader of the gay liberation movement. However, on November 27, 1978, he, along with Mayor George Moscone, was shot to death by fellow supervisor Dan White. His death was a clarion call for gays and lesbians across the nation to accelerate the fight for gay rights.*

*The following speech was delivered at the first Gay Freedom Day Parade in San Francisco on June 25, 1978. Milk refers to several of his archrivals at the time, including Anita Bryant of Florida, who launched a nationwide anti–gay rights crusade called Save Our Children, and California state senator John Briggs, who authored the Briggs Initiative to prohibit homosexuals from teaching in public schools. Milk attacks their campaigns, which portrayed gay people as child molesters. He also condemns then-president Jimmy Carter for ignoring gay rights as an important civil rights issue. The solution to antigay discrimination, says Milk, is for gay people to "come out" and publicly stand up for gay rights and for all disenfranchised groups to join together to demand human rights for all.*

Harvey Milk, speech at the first Gay Freedom Day Parade, San Francisco, June 25, 1978.

My name is Harvey Milk—and I want to recruit you. I want to recruit you for the fight to preserve your democracy from the John Briggs and the Anita Bryants who are trying to constitutionalize bigotry. We are not going to allow that to happen. We are not going to sit back in silence as 300,000 of our gay brothers and sisters did in Nazi Germany. We are not going to allow our rights to be taken away and then march with bowed heads into the gas chambers. On this anniversary of [the Stonewall riots that launched the gay rights movement] I ask my gay sisters and brothers to make the commitment to fight. For themselves. For their freedom. For their country.

## In Our City

Here, in San Francisco, we recently held an election for a judgeship. An anti-gay smear campaign was waged against a presiding judge because she was supported by lesbians and gay men. Here, in so-called liberal San Francisco, an anti-gay smear campaign was waged by so-called liberals.

And here, in so-called liberal San Francisco, we have a columnist for the *San Francisco Examiner*, a columnist named Kevin Starr, who has printed a number of columns containing distortions and lies about gays. He's getting away with it.

These anti-gay smear campaigns, these anti-gay columns, are laying the groundwork for the Briggs initiative [that would prohibit homosexuals from teaching in public schools]. We had better be prepared for it.

In the *Examiner*, Kevin Starr defames and libels gays. In the *San Francisco Chronicle*, Charles McCabe warns us to be quiet, that talking about gay rights is *counter-productive*. To Mr. McCabe I say that the day he stops talking about freedom of the press is the day he no longer has it.

The blacks did not win their rights by sitting quietly in the back of the bus. They got off!

Gay people, we will not win [our] rights by staying quietly in our closets. . . . We are coming out! We are coming out to fight the lies, the myths, the distortions! We are coming out to tell the truth about gays!

*For I'm tired of the conspiracy of silence.* I'm tired of listening to the Anita Bryants twist the language and the meaning of the bible to fit their own distorted outlook. But I'm even more tired of the *silence* from the religious leaders of this nation who *know* that she is playing fast and loose with the true meaning of the bible. *I'm tired of their silence more than of her biblical gymnastics!*

And I'm tired of John Briggs talking about false role models. He's lying in his teeth and he knows it. But I'm even more tired of the silence from educators and psychologists who know that Briggs is lying and yet say nothing. *I'm tired of their silence more than of Briggs' lies!*

## Myths and Facts

I'm tired of the silence so I'm going to talk about it. And I want *you* to talk about it.

*Gay people, we are painted as child molesters.* I want to talk about that. I want to talk about the *myth* of child molestations by gays. I want to talk about the *fact* that in this state some 95 percent of child molestations are heterosexual and usually the parent. . . .

I want to talk about the *fact* that all child abandonments are heterosexual.

I want to talk about the *fact* that all abuse of children is by their heterosexual parents.

I want to talk about the *fact* that some 98 percent of the six million rapes committed annually are heterosexual.

I want to talk about the *fact* that one out of every three women who will be murdered in this state this year will be murdered by their husbands.

I want to talk about the *fact* that some 30 percent of all marriages contain domestic violence.

And finally, I want to tell the John Briggs and the Anita Bryants that *you* talk about the *myths* of gays but today *I'm* talking about the *facts* of *heterosexual violence* and what

the hell are you going to do about that?????
*Clean up your own house before you start telling lies about gays. Don't distort the bible to hide your own sins. Don't change facts to lies. Don't look for cheap political advantage in playing upon people's fears! Judging by the latest polls, even the youth can tell you're lying!*

Anita Bryant, John Briggs: your unwillingness to talk about your own house, your deliberate lies and distortions, your unwillingness to face the truth, chills my blood—it reeks of madness!

## Are They Our Allies?

And like the rest of you, *I'm tired* of our so-called friends who tell us that we must set standards.

What standards?

The standards of the rapists? The wife beaters? The child abusers? The people who ordered the bomb to be built? The people who ordered it to be dropped? The people who pulled the trigger? The people who gave us Vietnam? The people who built the gas chambers? The people who built the concentration camps—right *here* in California, and then herded all the Japanese-Americans into them during World War II. . . . The Jew baiters? The nigger knockers? The corporate thiefs? The Nixons? The Hitlers?

What standards do *you* want *us* to set? Clean up your act, clean up your violence before you criticize lesbians and gay men because of their sexuality. . . . It is *madness* to glorify killing and violence on one hand and be ashamed of the sexual act, the act that conceived you, on the other. . . .

*There is a difference between morality and murder.* The *fact* is that more people have been slaughtered in the name of religion than for any other single reason. That, that, my friends, *that is true perversion!* For the standards that we should set, should we read your next week's headlines? . . .

Well, I'm tired of the lies of the Anita Bryants and the John Briggs.

I'm tired of their myths.

I'm tired of their distortions.
I'm speaking out about it.

## Come Out Now!

Gay brothers and sisters, what are *you* going to do about it? You must *come out*. Come out . . . to your parents . . . I know that it is hard and will hurt them but think about how they will *hurt you* in the voting booth! *Come out . . . to your relatives.* I know that is hard and will upset them but think of how they will *upset you* in the voting booth. *Come out to your friends* . . . if indeed they are your friends. *Come out* to your neighbors . . . to your fellow workers . . . to the people *who work* where you eat and shop. . . . *Come out* only to the people you know, *and who know you.* Not to anyone else. But once and for all, break down the myths, destroy the lies and distortions.

For your sake.
*For their sake.*

For the sake of the *youngsters* who are becoming scared by the votes from Dade [County, Florida] to Eugene [Oregon].

If Briggs wins he will not stop. They never do. Like all mad people, they are forced to go on, to *prove* they were right!

There will be no safe "closet" for any gay person.

So break out of yours today—tear the damn thing down once and for all!

And finally
Most of all
*I'm tired* of the *silence* from the White House.

## President Jimmy Carter

Jimmy Carter, you talked about human rights a lot. . . . In fact, you want to be the world's leader for human rights. *Well, damn it, lead!!!* There are some fifteen to twenty million lesbians and gay men in this nation listening and listening very carefully.

Jimmy Carter, when are you going to talk about *their* rights?

You talk a lot about the bible. . . . But when are you going to talk about that most important part: "Love thy neighbor?" After all, she may be gay.

Jimmy Carter, the time has come for lesbians and gay men to come out—and they are. Now the time has come for you to speak out. When are you?

Until you speak out against hatred, bigotry, madness, you are just Jimmy Carter. When you do, then and only then, will some twenty million lesbians and gay men be able to say Jimmy Carter is *our* president, too!

Jimmy Carter, you have the choice: *How many more years?*

*How much more damage?*

*How much more violence?*

*How many more lives?*

*History says that, like all groups seeking their rights, sooner or later we will win.*

*The question is: When?*

*Jimmy Carter, you have to make the choice—it's in your hands: either years of violence . . . or you can help turn the pages of history that much faster.*

## March on Washington

*It is up to you. And now, before it becomes too late, come to California and speak out against Briggs. . . .*

*If you don't—then we will come to you!!! If you do not speak out, if you remain silent. If you do not lift your voice against Briggs, then I call upon lesbians and gay men from all over the nation . . . your nation . . . to gather in Washington . . . one year from now . . . on that national day of freedom, the fourth of July. . . . the fourth of July, 1979 . . . to gather in Washington on that very same spot where over a decade ago Dr. Martin Luther King spoke to a nation of his dreams . . . dreams that are fast fading, dreams that to many millions in the nation have become nightmares rather than dreams. . . .*

I call upon all minorities and especially the millions of lesbians and gay men to wake up from their dreams. . . . To gather in Washington and tell Jimmy Carter and their nation: "Wake up . . . wake up, America . . . no more racism, no more sexism, no more ageism, no more hatred . . . no more!"

It's up to you, Jimmy Carter. . . . Do you want to go down in history as a person who would not listen . . . or do you want to go down in history as a leader, as a president?

Jimmy Carter, listen to us today . . . or you will have to listen to lesbians and gay men from all over this nation as they gather in Washington next year. . . .

For we *will* gather there and we will tell you about America and what it really stands for. . . .

*And to the bigots . . . to the John Briggs . . . to the Anita Bryants . . . to the Kevin Starrs and all their ilk. . . . Let me remind you what America is . . . listen carefully:*

*On the Statue of Liberty it says: "Give me your tired, your poor, your huddled masses, yearning to be free. . . ." In the Declaration of Independence it is written: "All men are created equal and they are endowed with certain inalienable rights. . . ." And in our national anthem it says: "Oh, say does that Star-Spangled Banner yet wave o'er the land of the free."*

For Mr. Briggs and Mrs. Bryant and Mr. Starr and *all* the bigots out there: *That's what America is. No matter how hard you try, you cannot erase those words from the Declaration of Independence. No matter how hard you try, you cannot chip those words from off the base of the Statue of Liberty. And no matter how hard [you try] you cannot sing the "Star Spangled Banner" without those words.*

That's what America is.

Love it or leave it.

# AIDS Activists Are Spreading Dangerous Myths About AIDS

*FIRST THINGS*

*The following selection was first published in the conservative periodical* First Things: The Journal of Religion, Culture, and Public Life *in 1992. It disputes many of the claims made by gay rights and AIDS activists at that time. The article accuses gay AIDS activists of using dangerous propaganda to dissociate AIDS from homosexual behavior. The authors contend that because the majority of AIDS victims are homosexual, obviously homosexual activity and promiscuity perpetuate the epidemic. Those involved in AIDS campaigns want to gain social acceptance of homosexuality and transcend morality altogether, the article argues.* First Things *is published by the Institute on Religion and Public Life, an interreligious research and education institute whose purpose is to advance religiously informed public philosophies and policies.*

R eaders whose minds have not been numbed by all the media-generated sensations since then may be able to recall that back in the first part of November [1991] the nation was reportedly held in thrall by Magic Johnson's announcement that he had the AIDS virus. More than one television anchor solemnly announced that the country

*First Things*, "AIDS: Deadly Confusions Compounded," vol. 20, February 1992. Copyright © 1992 by the Institute on Religion and Public Life. Reproduced by permission.

had not been so traumatized since the assassination of John F. Kennedy. The good news was that Magic, a "role model" for America's youth, was going to spend his remaining days advocating safe (some said safer) sex.

To their credit, within a few days some reporters challenged the idea that Johnson was an exemplar for America's young, and especially for blacks. Off the court where he did his magic for the Los Angeles Lakers, Johnson had dropped out of college, fathered at least one child out of wedlock, and led a sexual life that is politely termed promiscuous. Magic was "my role model," says Wilt Chamberlain, who brags, perhaps preposterously, that he has slept with 20,000 women over the years. In the face of Johnson's charm and high spirits in making his announcement, some journalists were impertinent enough to wonder how many women whom Johnson infected would die of AIDS. Proponents of the homosexual cause were vocally upset that Johnson made clear he is heterosexual, thus reminding people of the ill-disguised connection between AIDS transmission and the "gay lifestyle." (Later, to his credit, Johnson had a change of mind and said he would be urging unmarried people to abstain from sex rather than practice "safe sex." He told reporters, "What I'm trying to do is save lives.")

## AIDS Propaganda

The incessantly repeated line of the AIDS industry is that this is a disease that is out of control (a "pandemic") and that everybody is at risk of contracting it. But of course that is not true. As documented by Michael Fumento (*The Myth of Heterosexual AIDS*, New Republic Books) and by Ronald Brookmeyer of Johns Hopkins, the epidemic is declining among all risk categories. (See "AIDS So Fat," *Commentary*, December 1991). Since it erupted ten years ago, 188,348 cases have been reported in the United States, with 121,196 ending in death. The risk is far from being equally distributed. Propaganda to the contrary notwithstanding, AIDS is most emphatically a respecter of persons, or at least of behaviors. A mere 727 whites, middle-class or otherwise, are listed as having contracted the disease through heterosexual contact—less than one-half of one percent of the total caseload.

In the same period that 121,00 died of AIDS, more than four times as many Americans have died in car accidents and fifty times as many have died of cancer. The point of such a comparison is not to downplay the tragedy of AIDS but to underscore the fatuity of the repeated claim that America is "not paying attention to the AIDS crisis." In terms of media notice, as well as private and government funding, AIDS is receiving attention wildly disproportionate to its place in the constellation of health problems facing the American people. Given the sector of the population that is chiefly at risk, that is not entirely surprising. Those afflicted with HIV or AIDS in the homosexual subculture are mainly young, often talented, concentrated in media-sensitive occupations, urban, affluent, and politically vocal. That is a potent combination and helps explain why a horrible disease breaking out among those who engage in certain sexual practices has actually resulted in increased public sympathy for the practitioners.

The AIDS lobby believes that sustaining such sympathy requires that they belittle or deny the connection between AIDS and homosexual practice. It is an article of faith with them that ours is a "homophobic" society. Thus *New York Times* columnist Anna Quindlen: "Over the last year we have witnessed the canonization of one AIDS patient, a 23-year-old woman named Kimberly Bergalis who says that she 'didn't do anything wrong.' This is code, and so is her elevation to national symbol. Kimberly Bergalis is a lovely white woman with no sexual history who contracted AIDS from her dentist. She is what some people like to call 'an innocent victim.'" (Kimberly Bergalis has since died.) To Ms. Quindlen and those who think like her, it is intolerable that we think there are innocent victims. It might lead to the conclusion that there are victims who are something other than innocent, and therefore perhaps not "victims" at all. Sympathy, however, should not have to depend upon mendacity.

AIDS is, in the jargon of the social scientists, behavior-specific. Of AIDS cases in America, 66 percent are homosexuals and 22 percent are intravenous drug users infected by homosexuals. Six percent are wives, lovers, or babies of people with AIDS. In sum, the AIDS epidemic in America is a product of homosexual activity, notably anal intercourse between men. Those in the schools who teach children that the lesson to be drawn is that "it could happen to anyone," that everyone is equally at risk, are simply lying. Teachers should not lie to their students, but most programs in AIDS education are doing precisely that. The lie is compounded by the constant contention that the answer to the crisis is government action. That routinely means increased government funding, but it is also said that President [George] Bush and other national leaders should "speak out" on the crisis.

What on earth can the critics want? Perhaps the President should go on prime time to warn people against patterns of behavior that more than 120,000 deaths have not effectively discouraged. Or maybe there should be a law against athletes such as Magic Johnson taking the groupies that hang around the locker rooms back to their hotels. Vice President [Dan] Quayle has had the temerity to speak out on AIDS. He suggests that an answer to AIDS might be abstinence. For this he is roundly reviled. Worse than not speaking out on AIDS is to speak out in a way that violates the studied pretense that AIDS is not a behavior-specific disease.

The first rule is to abstain from sex or have sex only with a faithful spouse, the second is not to use intravenous drugs. In addition, do not receive infected blood, avoid being operated on by health workers with AIDS, and somehow manage not to be born to parents with the disease. Follow those rules and you have, on the basis of everything that is known, zero chance of contracting AIDS. Follow the first two and you have much less chance of getting AIDS than of being killed in an airplane crash. Such are the relatively simple facts that a massive program of deception called "AIDS education" is designed to obscure.

## Ulterior Motives

Admittedly, deception is a hard word. Are we impugning the motives of those involved in this program? Yes, it does seem to come down to that, at least in many cases. No doubt there are people involved who have no desire other than to reduce the incidence of AIDS. But it would be disingenuous to deny that those who orchestrate the AIDS campaign have various other purposes in mind. This is not an accusation, for they typically do not deny it, indeed they are volubly articulate about those purposes.

At least three purposes are obvious. For some, the goal is to rescue the sexual revolution that began some three decades ago and is, in their view, one of the great progressive achievements of the century. For some, the goal is to gain social acceptance of homosexuality as an alternative lifestyle, on a par with or superior to marriage between men and women. For some, the goal is to transcend morality altogether, especially religiously grounded morality, and to create a "liberated" society of freedom unbounded in which all unpleasant consequences are amenable to a technical fix. And some embrace all three goals.

Those who embrace these goals have an enormous stake in managing very carefully the public discussion of the AIDS epidemic. They recognize that more and more people have come to the conclusion that the sexual revolution turned out to be a bust. Disease, abortion, illegitimacy, child neglect, sexual abuse, and divorce—especially men "trading in" for younger wives—have all increased sharply. The sexual revolution has simply failed in its promise to make people happy, and for many Americans that is the highest, if not the only, test of morality. For many others it has brought nothing but anxiety, domestic disaster, and, in the case of people with AIDS, death. And yet, for the true believers in what they proclaim as the defining achievement of their generation there can be, as they say, no turning back of the clock on the sexual revolution. That is exactly what the AIDS epidemic threatened to do. By dint of skillful management, backed by lavish funding and media collaboration, the threat has been held at bay and even turned to the advantage of the revolution. That is no small accomplishment.

## The Dangers in Promoting Condom Use

For the proponents of homosexuality and an amoral society in which every consequence is mended by a technical fix, the chief response to the AIDS crisis is the promotion of condoms. Much attention has been paid the distribution, without parental permission, of condoms to the school children of New York City. While the political leadership of this city is certifiably madder than most, it is reported that at least sixteen school districts around the country have similar plans in the works and are watching the New York "experiment" with great interest. Critics of the program protest that it is a despair-based policy which assumes that adolescents and teenagers—especially blacks and Hispanics—are rutting animals, and the only thing to be done is to encourage them to rut more safely.

The critics are right, of course. All the studies indicate that most teenagers, including minority teenagers, are not "sexually active," if sexually active means indulging in promiscuous sex on a regular basis. According to the Department of Health and Human Services, 73 percent of fifteen-year-old girls in America are virgins. Fifty percent are virgins at age seventeen. The critics say that public policy should be based on strengths rather than pathologies, that it should aim at encouraging young people to follow the example of those who practice abstinence and chastity. They claim that handing out free condoms "sends the signal" that promiscuity is the normal thing. In fact, the program does not just send that signal: its promoters explicitly state that regular sex is the normal thing. They say in the program's defense that it also acknowledges abstinence as an option for those who choose it. They do not wish to be intolerant of those who, for whatever strange reason, decide not to be "sexually active." As right as the critics are on the facts, their argument misses the point. The point is that those who would salvage the sexual revolution believe that chastity and abstinence are unnatural and unhealthy. Virginity, in that view, is a form of sexual deviance.

There is a marvelous irony in the promotion of condoms. Not long ago it was argued that easy access to abortion is necessary because of the notorious failure rate of condoms. Experts claim that condoms fail 14 percent of the time, even when used according to directions. If any other consumer product was so flawed, [consumer advocate] Ralph Nader and his like would insist that it be banned. The National Commission on AIDS has established an 800 number where youngsters can get instruction on the proper use of condoms. The two-minute message lists six steps. Presumably kids (many of whom can hardly read or write) will take notes and carry the instructions with them at all times. The last instruction is that it is very important "to withdraw the penis before ejaculation." So we are back to old-fashioned *coitus interruptus.* The technical fix for the AIDS crisis is to have adolescents and teenagers at the peak of passionate abandon take out their list of rules, follow them assiduously, and then withdraw before climax. Anyone who says this scheme has any connection with the real world is either a liar or almost incredibly stupid.

## Gay-Controlled Sex Education

Yet there is purpose in the madness. It keeps alive the dogma of the sexual revolution that says regular sexual intercourse is necessary and healthy, and it provides great opportunity for spreading the message of the joy of homosexual sex. An official publication of the New York Public Schools, issued in the name of Joseph A. Fernandez, Chancellor, is titled "Resource Directory of Groups Providing HIV/AIDS Education to Schools." The first resource listed is ACT-UP (AIDS Coalition to Unleash Power), the group that uses brownshirt tactics to break up meetings of which it disapproves and, perhaps most infamously, desecrates the Mass at St. Patrick's Cathedral. Another resource listed is Gay Men's Health Crisis (GMHC), a somewhat less militant homosexual activist group. Other resources listed are equally committed to the homosexualist agenda.

According to the publication, these groups will supply teachers and students "with prompt support and accurate information." In short, active homosexuals who are self-described as advocates of the gay lifestyle are, under the auspices of the school system, counseling boys on the use of condoms for sexual fun and satisfaction—with safety in mind, of course. Those in charge of the program insist that condoms not be handed out willy-nilly; distribution must be accompanied by appropriate instruction. Homosexual organizations promptly volunteered to provide instructors, and the offer was readily accepted. It is not too much to say that the public schools have become an institutional procurer for the recruitment of school boys to the homosexual subculture, which in this city is less and less a *sub*culture. Little wonder that the champions of the condom program were adamant about eliminating any provisions for parental notification or consent. Little wonder that in the public hearings preceding the program's adoption the most vocal organized support was from the homosexual activists, loudly led by ACT-UP. At city hall, aides do not bother to deny that Mayor Dinkins' backing for the program was a matter of paying off a political debt to the homosexual activists without whose support he would not have been elected.

## A Death Sentence

Only the children of the poor are so vulnerable to the designs of the sexual revolutionists. In New York City, with extremely few exceptions, people who can afford an alternative do not send their children to the public schools. The result is that there is a racialist, if not racist, component to the "AIDS education" program. The message is clear: black and Hispanic youngsters are not capable of the self-restraint expected of others. And again, behind that message is the assumption that, for everyone, self-restraint is unnatural and unhealthy. As one activist at the condom hearings said, "We're going to give public school kids the opportunities denied other kids in this uptight, homophobic society." Some opportunities. The sadness is deepened by the fact that a few key black churches have been enlisted in the program and, in the words of the *Times*, "now recognize that AIDS is not a moral but a medical problem."

The necessary consequence, we reluctantly conclude, is unambiguous. Homosexual activists, public school officials, politicians, and their allies in the media and some churches are, in the name of AIDS education, sentencing an indeterminate number of young people to a horrible death. Some are culpably ignorant, others know perfectly well what they are doing. In the words of the late Abraham Joshua Heschel, "Some are guilty, all are responsible." And Americans who think that this enormity is limited to places such as New York City and San Francisco have not begun to understand the culture that, absent a revival of moral sanity, their children will inherit.

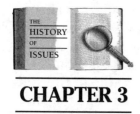

THE
HISTORY
OF
ISSUES

**CHAPTER 3**

# Legal and Legislative Battles

# Chapter Preface

A fter the historic 1969 Stonewall uprising in New York, slogans such as "Gay Power!" and "Come Out Now!" chanted by activists marked a clear departure from the polite and nonconfrontational tactics of activists in the 1950s and 1960s. By 1970 the new spirit of liberation inspired many gays and lesbians to march in the streets, openly celebrate gay and lesbian pride, and demand equal legal protection. No longer satisfied with the tamer rhetoric of homophile politics, organizations called for militant action as a necessary tool to effect change. Hundreds of gay liberation organizations formed, and gay publications skyrocketed, fostering a deeper sense of community and power. The growth in gay liberation groups cultivated the participation of people with differing backgrounds, ethnicities, and viewpoints. Racial minorities and lesbians insisted that their voices be heard along with those of middle-class white men who had dominated the gay rights movement in earlier decades.

This more inclusive and radical movement was put to the test when the AIDS epidemic began in the early 1980s. Thousands of gay men were entering hospitals with a strange and devastating illness that was dubbed the "gay cancer" or the Gay-Related Immune Deficiency Syndrome (GRIDS). When it became apparent that nongay people also contracted the syndrome, it was renamed Acquired Immune Deficiency Syndrome, or AIDS. AIDS changed the face of gay activism by the late 1980s. The disease radicalized the movement even further and changed its focus. In reaction to the apparent apathy of the government and the medical establishment to the fate of AIDS sufferers, many gay and lesbian activists began to demand that the U.S.

government dedicate resources to end the AIDS crisis.

The 1970s and 1980s were a time of increasing political strength for the gay liberation movement. Not surprisingly, the era was also characterized by the increasing political organization of those opposed to homosexuality and the gains that gay activists had made. The conflict between these two groups was carried into the 1990s and beyond.

# Protections for Homosexuals Must Be Fought to Protect the American Family

ANITA BRYANT

*Anita Bryant was a successful gospel and pop singer when she launched one of the most famous battles against gay rights during the 1970s. At the time she was well known in the United States as the spokesperson for the Florida Citrus Commission, regularly appearing in television commercials. When a gay rights ordinance was passed in her home county of Dade in Florida, which declared that housing, public accommodations, and employment rights could not be abridged on the basis of sexuality, she rose up as a born-again Christian mother to lead a campaign for its repeal. She claimed that homosexuals were godless and that gay teachers would try to recruit children into homosexuality. In the following selection she describes the event that inspired her to organize her Save Our Children crusade. She testified at the Dade County Board of Commissioners hearing concerning the pro–gay rights ordinance. As she explains, she was shocked when the ordinance passed despite strong opposition to it.*

*Bryant persevered, and the ordinance was ultimately repealed by a two-to-one margin on June 7, 1977. In the next few years she became a national leader of the growing resis-*

*tance to gay rights protections that had passed in over forty U.S. cities. However, soon after her victory in Miami she was fired by the Citrus Commission, largely because gays and lesbians mounted an effective and well-publicized boycott of Florida citrus. Her singing career fell apart shortly thereafter. The gay rights ordinance was reinstated in Dade County in 1999.*

The battle lines were drawn in Miami on that memorable cold January [1977] morning. The foot soldiers were housewives and mothers, religious and civic leaders in opposition to a well-organized, highly financed, and politically militant group of homosexual activists.

We emerged at the scene of the controversy as an unorganized but deeply concerned and committed group of parents and citizens upon whom had been foisted an ordinance[1] which was against everything we believed in and stood for. We had neither marshaled our defenses, nor had we developed a strategy as the leaders of the militant homosexual movement had obviously done. We had done our homework: We did know why we were there, but there was nothing political or militant in our motives. Most of us had never seen each other before, and our first introductions were at the courthouse.

As the nation was to see in succeeding weeks, our stand brought death threats, harassment, heartache, distortions of statements by the media, tremendous pressures, disruption of our private lives, and a host of problems we had not envisioned when we took our stand. For me, in addition to all of the above, it brought job discrimination and the loss of a lifelong dream of having a television show of my own. We were cast as bigots, haters, discriminators, and deniers

---

1. The ordinance amended Chapter 11A of the Dade County (Florida) Code to prohibit discrimination in housing, public accommodation, and employment against persons based on their affectional or sexual preference.

of basic human rights. And all of this happened because we were sincerely concerned for our children and our community.

I felt strong, confident, and at peace. I had carefully studied the wording of the amendment. I knew the Scriptures. My own personal preparation for the confrontation was complete. People were praying. We had prayed, and even while we were in that hearing, the Lord was reading my heart and hearing the cries welling up from deep within me. I knew God's hand was upon us.

The local "gay" activists were there with those who had joined them in their defense of the ordinance. Under the banner of the Dade County Coalition for the Humanistic Rights of Gays, they flexed their political muscles. While much of the media and sympathizers to the homosexuals were shouting about discrimination, the spokesman for the local group admitted at the hearing that homosexuals as individuals *are* able to obtain housing, employment, and education without discrimination in Dade County. "We are there now and what we want to do is tell you where we're at," their avowed leader said.

"If there is no discrimination, then there is no need for this ordinance," said Mayor Steve Clark.

We outnumbered the opposition by eight to one at the hearing, even though they brought in some speakers from out of state. Homosexuals in Dade County had made a discovery during the local elections the preceding year—they discovered they had political clout. Dade County became another testing ground for them in their continuing nationwide efforts to gain so-called rights and life-style approval. This was to be proved in the months ahead as political organizers from around the country joined them in launching a full-fledged crusade.

Proponents of the ordinance framed the issue as civil rights versus bigotry. Nothing could have been further from the truth. At the hearing, the leaders of the homosexual movement had their say first. When it came time for those of us who opposed the ordinance to speak, some very articulate religious and civic leaders in the community presented views which we felt validated our stand and would compel the Metro Commission to reverse its original vote.

## Speaking Out

Reverend Charles Couey from South Dade Baptist Church was the first man called on to speak for our side. There was an immediately noticeable hush throughout the room as this man of God stood with only the Word of God in his hands and, without expounding or explaining the Scripture in any way, read from the first chapter of Romans.

> Professing themselves to be wise, they became fools. And changed the glory of the uncorruptible God into an image made like to corruptible man, and to birds, and fourfooted beasts, and creeping things. Wherefore God also gave them up to uncleanness, through the lusts of their own hearts, to dishonour their own bodies between themselves: Who changed the truth of God into a lie, and worshipped and served the creature more than the Creator, who is blessed for ever. Amen.

> For this cause God gave them up unto vile affections: for even their women did change the natural use into that which is against nature: And likewise also the men, leaving the natural use of the woman, burned in their lust one toward another; men with men working that which is unseemly, and receiving in themselves that recompence of their error which was meet.

> And even as they did not like to retain God in their knowledge, God gave them over to a reprobate mind, to do those things which are not convenient; Being filled with all unrighteousness, fornication, wickedness, covetousness, maliciousness; full of envy, murder, debate, deceit, malignity; whisperers, backbiters, haters of God, despiteful, proud, boasters, inventors of evil things, disobedient to parents, without understanding, covenantbreakers, without natural affection, implaca-

ble, unmerciful: Who knowing the judgment of God, that they which commit such things are worthy of death, not only do the same, but have pleasure in them that do them.

Romans 1:22–32

The Roman Catholic Church, through its attorney, prominent Miamian Joseph Fitzgerald, said the ordinance would permit known practicing homosexuals to teach in private church schools and to act as role models for their pupils, showing that homosexuality is an acceptable and respectable alternative to the life-style of the children's parents. This, he said, would be directly counter to teachings of the Catholic Church. Later, Archbishop Coleman Carroll, prestigious leader of South Florida's heavy Catholic population and its fifty-six schools, said the Church would refuse to obey the law and would oppose it vigorously in the courts.

These comments were particularly significant in view of the fact that, by a peculiarity of the Dade County charter, the Metro Commission has no authority over the large public-school population of the county, the sixth largest in the nation. The new homosexual license would have applied solely to private and religious schools. In Dade County there are more than a hundred such schools: Jewish, Protestant, secular, and Catholic.

Robert M. Brake, a Coral Gables city commissioner and a former Metro Commissioner, said the ordinance was a bad law and maintained that homosexuals were already granted all rights against discrimination under existing federal laws. This effort, he said, was a carefully disguised attempt to break down further the moral fabric of society. He said the law would give these people special privileges that would only be to the detriment of society in general and children in particular.

Alvin Dark, former manager of the champion Oakland A's and now manager of the San Diego Padres, simply opened his Bible and gave the plan of salvation for *any* sinner.

# My Turn

When it was my turn to speak, I addressed the mayor and members of the commission with these words:

I come here today with no prejudice in my heart, no hate, no anger, or judgment against my fellowman. But I do come with a deep burden for my country, my community, and my children's well-being.

The commissioners have already received my letter and know full well my stand as a Christian, and I make no apologies for that.

I'm speaking to you today not as an entertainer who has worked with homosexuals all my life—and I have never discriminated against them; I have a policy of live and let live as long as they do not discriminate against me. But I am a wife and a mother, and I especially address you today as a mother. I have a God-given right to be jealous of the moral environment for my children.

I remind you that the God who made us could have made us like the sea turtle who comes in the dark of night and buries her eggs in the sand and never cares about her children again. But God created us so our children would be dependent upon us as their parents for their lives. And I, for one, will do everything I can as a citizen, as a Christian, and especially as a mother to insure that they have the right to a healthy and morally good life.

The cry of work discrimination has been the key that has unlocked the door of freedom to *legitimate* minority groups; now, it is time to recognize the rights of the overwhelming majority of Dade County who are being discriminated against because they have the right to say no. Just when did the word *discrimination* start meaning "I can't say no"? The people of Dade County can't say no now in the areas of housing, employment, and education. But I can, and I do say no to a very serious moral issue that would violate my rights and the rights of all decent and morally upstanding citizens, regardless of their race or religion.

We urge the Dade County Commissioners to act responsibly for the vast majority of their constituents. . . .

Because we were not organized, Orthodox Rabbi Phineas Weberman did not get to speak, but he did present his statement to the commissioners afterwards. He said his five-thousand-year-old religion had always condemned homosexuality as unnatural, unproductive, sinful, and a flagrant violation of God's laws and the laws of the vast majority of mankind in all ages.

And there were others who spoke out against the ordinance that day. We all agreed that we were opposed to their demands for what they considered a basic "right" and the affirmation by society that what they were doing was right. But our voices were united in protest. It was not solely a religious issue, as our opponents kept insisting; it was a moral issue on which society has a right to make its own contrary judgment.

Of course we were naive enough to think our presence and testimony were going to sway the commissioners. Had it been an actual court trial, the case would have been thrown out because the only reason for proposing the amendment was to show discrimination where there was none.

Immediately after hearing arguments from both sides, the commission voted. The measure was passed by a five-to-three vote, setting up what had to be an inevitable future confrontation. The fight was not over. The commission majority included Ruth Shack, Bill Oliver, James Redford, Beverly Phillips, and Harvey Ruvin. Opponents included Metro Mayor Steve Clark and Commissioners Clara Oesterle and Neal Adams. Barry Schreiber was absent because of illness.

## Shock and Disappointment

I was visibly stunned, as were the others. I couldn't believe it. I was devastated. I sat there, and I heard the result of the vote, and I thought, *This is a free country, and if we present our case and we're right and if it's proven, then we should win it.*

That's what shocked me so badly—to think we live in a country where freedom and right are supposed to reign, a country that boasts "In God we trust" and has such a rich spiritual heritage; yet where internal decadence is all too evident, where the Word of God and the voice of the majority is sometimes not heeded at all. Has it come to this: that we are a society that in fact does glorify aberrant behavior and oppresses the rights of the majority on a moral issue? I was not the only one in the room that day who was thoroughly disillusioned.

Suddenly the TV cameras started rolling and zeroing in. "Who's your leader?"; "How do you feel?"; "Are you disappointed?"

"Yes," I said, "I'm disappointed, and I'm shaken, but the flame that God put in my heart is becoming a torch. It will not be quenched. We have just begun to fight."

I was aflame with indignation. The Bible calls it "righteous anger."

Immediately following the vote, those of us who were in opposition met. There was a mixture of outrage and deep sadness. Some of us felt numb. Robert Brake stepped up and introduced himself. He said we needed to form an organized effort to defeat this ordinance by petition and referendum. We would need an organization. His next question was: "Would you head it up, Anita, as chairman?"

I turned to my husband, who was as outraged and disturbed as I, and we conferred. The answer, of course, had to be yes. There could be no turning back now. We still did not know, however, the repercussions that would be felt because of all this. I was quoted in the papers as saying, "Even if my livelihood is stripped away from me, I will not be moved. I'd rather have the love of God and be making this a better place to live for my children and other children." And I meant it. With all my heart I meant it then, and I mean it now.

I would give my life, if necessary, to protect my children.

I'm concerned about giving them the right food and meeting all their physical needs, but if I let up on their spiritual welfare, what good is it?

## Dealing with the Media

The media misquoted me, saying that I called homosexuals *garbage*. That was not what I said. As I talked about our concern for the health and diet of our children and other people's children, I said, "If they are exposed to homosexuality, I might as well feed them garbage." I think there is a difference, but I leave it to the reader to interpret as you wish—we did not resort to name-calling at any time during the campaign in Miami.

Criticism from the media was an eye-opener for me. We were quoted and misquoted time after time. A case in point is an interview I had with the religion editor of the Orlando *Sentinel-Star*. I quoted the familiar 1 Corinthians 6:9 passage which lists the "unrighteous [who] shall not inherit the kingdom of God." I said to her that murderers, drunkards, thieves, homosexuals, and *all* who have not turned from their sin are included as needing to be repentant. The headline in the paper read: ANITA BRYANT CALLS HOMOSEXUALS MURDERERS!

There were all kinds of lies and distortions including one in particular which concerned a bumper sticker which allegedly said: KILL A QUEER FOR CHRIST. May the Lord strike me dead if I or any member of Save Our Children had anything to do with such a supposed bumper sticker. To this date I have yet to find one person who has even seen such a sticker. This happened over and over again.

But we stood strong in our defense against what we saw as encroaching moral decay in America, and in our own city and county in particular. Hundreds of newspaper and magazine clippings came our way; the comments ranged from my being accused of sounding a homophobic pitch to being called "a courageous woman."

As we stood outside the courtroom chambers, we knew

we had to face this moral crisis. Later on I knew, from information that had been sent to me, that in California this same kind of battle had been fought and all but lost due to the apathy of the public. With the help of our local religious and civic leaders, I sensed that we as wives and mothers had to march out of our living rooms and fight for the repeal of this ordinance. I joined with Judi Wilson and others who emphasized, "This is not a hate campaign. We're motivated because we love our children, our nation, and our country. And we have love and concern for homosexuals, too."

# Antisodomy Laws Are Constitutional

BYRON WHITE

*On the night of August 2, 1982, an Atlanta bartender named Michael Hardwick was arrested under a Georgia antisodomy statute after he was found engaging in oral sex with another man. Antisodomy laws, some dating back to colonial times, were still on record in many states, criminalizing many sexual activities that were associated with homosexuality. The county prosecutor decided to drop the case for lack of evidence. However, resistance to antisodomy laws had been growing along with the gay rights movement, and many felt it was time to challenge them. With the help of the American Civil Liberties Union (ACLU), Hardwick brought suit in the federal district court against Georgia attorney general Michael J. Bowers to challenge the constitutionality of the Georgia law. The case went all the way to the U.S. Supreme Court, which ruled against Hardwick, delivering a blow to the gay rights movement. Although the Court traditionally supported the constitutional right to privacy in relation to sexual activity, five out of nine justices in the* Bowers v. Hardwick *case upheld the Georgia antisodomy statute. In the next selection Justice Byron White explains the majority opinion for the Court.*

After being charged with violating the Georgia statute criminalizing sodomy by committing that act with another adult male in the bedroom of his home, respondent Hardwick (respondent) brought suit in Federal District Court, challenging the constitutionality of the statute insofar as it criminalized consensual sodomy. The court granted

Byron White, opinion, *Bowers v. Hardwick*, U.S. Supreme Court, Washington, DC, June 1986.

the defendants' motion to dismiss for failure to state a claim. The Court of Appeals reversed and remanded, holding that the Georgia statute violated respondent's fundamental rights.

*Held:*

The Georgia statute is constitutional.

(a) The Constitution does not confer a fundamental right upon homosexuals to engage in sodomy. None of the fundamental rights announced in this Court's prior cases involving family relationships, marriage, or procreation bear any resemblance to the right asserted in this case. And any claim that those cases stand for the proposition that any kind of private sexual conduct between consenting adults is constitutionally insulated from state proscription is unsupportable.

(b) Against a background in which many States have criminalized sodomy and still do, to claim that a right to engage in such conduct is "deeply rooted in this Nation's history and tradition" or "implicit in the concept of ordered liberty" is, at best, facetious.

(c) There should be great resistance to expand the reach of the Due Process Clauses to cover new fundamental rights. Otherwise, the Judiciary necessarily would take upon itself further authority to govern the country without constitutional authority. The claimed right in this case falls far short of overcoming this resistance.

(d) The fact that homosexual conduct occurs in the privacy of the home does not affect the result.

(e) Sodomy laws should not be invalidated on the asserted basis that majority belief that sodomy is immoral is an inadequate rationale to support the laws. . . .

## The Opinion of the Court[1]

In August 1982, respondent Hardwick (hereafter respondent) was charged with violating the Georgia statute crim-

1. The summary in the previous paragraphs is from the Web site SodomyLaws at www.sodomylaws.org/bowers/bowers_v_hardwick.htm. Justice Byron White's opinion begins here.

inalizing sodomy by committing that act with another adult male in the bedroom of respondent's home. After a preliminary hearing, the District Attorney decided not to present the matter to the grand jury unless further evidence developed.

Respondent then brought suit in the Federal District Court, challenging the constitutionality of the statute insofar as it criminalized consensual sodomy. He asserted that he was a practicing homosexual, that the Georgia sodomy statute, as administered by the defendants, placed him in imminent danger of arrest, and that the statute for several reasons violates the Federal Constitution. The District Court granted the defendants' motion to dismiss for failure to state a claim, relying on *Doe v. Commonwealth's Attorney for the City of Richmond*, which this Court summarily affirmed. . . .

A divided panel of the Court of Appeals for the Eleventh Circuit reversed. The court first held that, because *Doe* was distinguishable and in any event had been undermined by later decisions, our summary affirmance in that case did not require affirmance of the District Court. Relying on our decisions in *Griswold v. Connecticut, Eisenstadt v. Baird, Stanley v. Georgia,* and *Roe v. Wade,* the court went on to hold that the Georgia statute violated respondent's fundamental rights because his homosexual activity is a private and intimate association that is beyond the reach of state regulation by reason of the Ninth Amendment and the Due Process Clause of the Fourteenth Amendment. The case was remanded for trial, at which, to prevail, the State would have to prove that the statute is supported by a compelling interest and is the most narrowly drawn means of achieving that end.

Because other Courts of Appeals have arrived at judgments contrary to that of the Eleventh Circuit in this case, we granted the Attorney General's petition for certiorari questioning the holding that the sodomy statute violates the fundamental rights of homosexuals. We agree with petitioner that the Court of Appeals erred, and hence reverse its judgment.

This case does not require a judgment on whether laws against sodomy between consenting adults in general, or between homosexuals in particular, are wise or desirable. It raises no question about the right or propriety of state legislative decisions to repeal their laws that criminalize homosexual sodomy, or of state-court decisions invalidating those laws on state constitutional grounds. The issue presented is whether the Federal Constitution confers a fundamental right upon homosexuals to engage in sodomy and hence invalidates the laws of the many States that still make such conduct illegal and have done so for a very long time. The case also calls for some judgment about the limits of the Court's role in carrying out its constitutional mandate.

We first register our disagreement with the Court of Appeals and with respondent that the Court's prior cases have construed the Constitution to confer a right of privacy that extends to homosexual sodomy and for all intents and purposes have decided this case. The reach of this line of cases was sketched in *Carey v. Population Services International, Pierce v. Society of Sisters*, and *Meyer v. Nebraska*, were described as dealing with child rearing and education; *Prince v. Massachusetts*, with family relationships; *Skinner v. Oklahoma ex rel. Williamson*, with procreation; *Loving v. Virginia*, with marriage; *Griswold v. Connecticut* supra, and *Eisenstadt v. Baird*, supra, with contraception; and *Roe v. Wade*, with abortion. The latter three cases were interpreted as construing the Due Process Clause of the Fourteenth Amendment to confer a fundamental individual right to decide whether or not to beget or bear a child. . . .

Accepting the decisions in these cases and the above description of them, we think it evident that none of the rights announced in those cases bears any resemblance to the claimed constitutional right of homosexuals to engage in acts of sodomy that is asserted in this case. No connection between family, marriage, or procreation on the one hand and homosexual activity on the other has been demonstrated, either by the Court of Appeals or by respondent. Moreover, any claim that these cases nevertheless stand for the proposition that any kind of private sexual conduct between consenting adults is constitutionally insulated from state proscription is unsupportable. Indeed, the Court's opinion in *Carey* twice asserted that the privacy right, which the *Griswold* line of cases found to be one of the protections provided by the Due Process Clause, did not reach so far.

Precedent aside, however, respondent would have us announce, as the Court of Appeals did, a fundamental right to engage in homosexual sodomy. This we are quite unwilling to do. It is true that despite the language of the Due Process Clauses of the Fifth and Fourteenth Amendments, which appears to focus only on the processes by which life, liberty, or property is taken, the cases are legion in which those Clauses have been interpreted to have substantive content, subsuming rights that to a great extent are immune from federal or state regulation or proscription. Among such cases are those recognizing rights that have little or no textual support in the constitutional language. *Meyer, Prince*, and *Pierce* fall in this category, as do the privacy cases from *Griswold* to *Carey*.

Striving to assure itself and the public that announcing rights not readily identifiable in the Constitution's text involves much more than the imposition of the Justices' own choice of values on the States and the Federal Government, the Court has sought to identify the nature of the rights qualifying for heightened judicial protection. In *Palko v. Connecticut*, it was said that this category includes those fundamental liberties that are "implicit in the concept of ordered liberty," such that "neither liberty nor justice would exist if [they] were sacrificed." A different description of fundamental liberties appeared in *Moore v. East Cleveland*, where they are characterized as those liberties that are "deeply rooted in this Nation's history and tradition."

It is obvious to us that neither of these formulations would extend a fundamental right to homosexuals to engage in acts of consensual sodomy. Proscriptions against that conduct have ancient roots. See generally *Survey on the Constitutional Right to Privacy in the Context of Homosexual Activity.* Sodomy was a criminal offense at common law and was forbidden by the laws of the original 13 States when they ratified the Bill of Rights. In 1868, when the Fourteenth Amendment was ratified, all but 5 of the 37 States in the Union had criminal sodomy laws. In fact, until 1961, all 50 States outlawed sodomy, and today, 24 States and the District of Columbia continue to provide criminal penalties for sodomy performed in private and between consenting adults. Against this background, to claim that a right to engage in such conduct is "deeply rooted in this Nation's history and tradition" or "implicit in the concept of ordered liberty" is, at best, facetious.

Nor are we inclined to take a more expansive view of our authority to discover new fundamental rights imbedded in the Due Process Clause. The Court is most vulnerable and comes nearest to illegitimacy when it deals with judge-made constitutional law having little or no cognizable roots in the language or design of the Constitution. That this is so was painfully demonstrated by the face-off between the Executive and the Court in the 1930's, which resulted in the repudiation of much of the substantive gloss that the Court had placed on the Due Process Clauses of the Fifth and Fourteenth Amendments. There should be, therefore, great resistance to expand the substantive reach of those Clauses, particularly if it requires redefining the category of rights deemed to be fundamental. Otherwise, the Judiciary necessarily takes to itself further authority to govern the country without express constitutional authority. The claimed right pressed on us today falls far short of overcoming this resistance.

Respondent, however, asserts that the result should be different where the homosexual conduct occurs in the privacy of the home. He relies on *Stanley v. Georgia*, where the Court held that the First Amendment prevents conviction for possessing and reading obscene material in the privacy of one's home: "If the First Amendment means anything, it means that a State has no business telling a man, sitting alone in his house, what books he may read or what films he may watch."

*Stanley* did protect conduct that would not have been protected outside the home, and it partially prevented the enforcement of state obscenity laws; but the decision was firmly grounded in the First Amendment. The right pressed upon us here has no similar support in the text of the Constitution, and it does not qualify for recognition under the prevailing principles for construing the Fourteenth Amendment. Its limits are also difficult to discern. Plainly enough, otherwise illegal conduct is not always immunized whenever it occurs in the home. Victimless crimes, such as the possession and use of illegal drugs, do not escape the law where they are committed at home. *Stanley* itself recognized that its holding offered no protection for the possession in the home of drugs, firearms, or stolen goods. And if respondent's submission is limited to the voluntary sexual conduct between consenting adults, it would be difficult, except by fiat, to limit the claimed right to homosexual conduct while leaving exposed to prosecution adultery, incest, and other sexual crimes even though they are committed in the home. We are unwilling to start down that road.

Even if the conduct at issue here is not a fundamental right, respondent asserts that there must be a rational basis for the law and that there is none in this case other than the presumed belief of a majority of the electorate in Georgia that homosexual sodomy is immoral and unacceptable. This is said to be an inadequate rationale to support the law. The law, however, is constantly based on notions of morality, and if all laws representing essentially moral choices are to be invalidated under the Due Process Clause, the courts will be very busy indeed. Even respon-

dent makes no such claim, but insists that majority senti-
ments about the morality of homosexuality should be declared inadequate. We do not agree, and are unpersuaded
that the sodomy laws of some 25 States should be invalidated on this basis.

Accordingly, the judgment of the Court of Appeals is Reversed.

# The Military's "Don't Ask, Don't Tell" Policy Cannot Be Justified

RHONDA EVANS

*As a presidential candidate in 1992, Bill Clinton promised to repeal the ban barring homosexuals from serving in the military. However, when he took office in 1993 he softened his stance due to strong opposition from the military establishment and Congress. Supporters of the ban argued that the presence of homosexual soldiers could undermine morale and unit cohesiveness. Clinton's compromise, informally called the "don't ask, don't tell" policy, took effect in 1994. Recruits cannot be asked their sexual orientation, but evidence of homosexual conduct can be turned over to unit commanders for fact-finding investigations. Military personnel found to be engaging in homosexual activity are then separated from military service. The effectiveness of "don't ask, don't tell" has been under debate ever since its implementation. The next selection is an excerpt from sociologist Rhonda Evans's report for the Center for the Study of Sexual Minorities in the Military at the University of California–Santa Barbara. Evans's research shows that gay and lesbian soldiers can serve openly without disrupting morale or compromising national security. She concludes that the military's "don't ask, don't tell" policy cannot be justified.*

Throughout the U.S. military's history, its treatment of sexual minorities has varied both as medical and popular understandings about homosexuality have shifted and as the needs of the armed forces themselves have changed. Military regulations have moved increasingly away from criminal prosecution to the discharge of homosexual service members in response to changing views among medical professionals about the root causes of homosexuality. Within an institution that has officially prohibited the service of sexual minorities since the 1940s, however, the actual implementation of the ban has fluctuated across time and branch of service, as well as among commanders. During periods of war, rates of discharge have declined as manpower needs have increased. Numerous examples exist of gay and lesbian military personnel who have served with the knowledge of other colleagues and even commanders. Further, not only does a service member's chance of being discharged vary by branch of service, but female service members also comprise a disproportionate number of those separated under the policy. Department of Defense officials have acknowledged in the past decade that the ban on homosexual service members has not resulted in the complete removal of gays and lesbians from the military and that many sexual minorities have served honorably in the U.S. armed forces. However, they continue to maintain that a removal of the ban would negatively affect morale, unit cohesion, and operational effectiveness within the U.S. military.

This report examines the development of, and reasoning behind, U. S. military policies restricting the service of homosexual men and women. It further analyzes scholarly, military, and governmental data concerning gay and lesbian service members and their effects on military operations. Studies of homosexual military personnel, foreign militaries, and domestic police and fire departments have consistently indicated that gay and lesbian service members can be successfully integrated into military and paramilitary organizations. . . . Collectively, they have served more than 18 years as openly homosexual military personnel. While these cases offer additional examples of exemplary service by homosexual service members, they also detail the responses of heterosexual personnel to extended service with openly homosexual military officers. Such case studies are meant to add nuance and detail to the quantitative research that has been established over the last fifty years, which have failed to measure any negative effect of the service of sexual minorities on the morale, unit cohesion, or operational effectiveness of military units. These service members in the four case studies maintained collegial relations with their co-workers, and they received promotions, medals and commendations, exemplary evaluations, and continued high levels of responsibility during their periods of open service. . . .

During the 1992 presidential campaign, then-candidate [Bill] Clinton vowed to "lift the ban" on sexual minorities serving in the military. Clinton's vow created a firestorm of opposition among the Joint Chiefs of Staff, Armed Services Committee Chair Sam Nunn, and other members of Congress, and opponents mobilized immediately to block the president's efforts. On January 29, 1993, President Clinton instructed the secretary of defense to draft an "Executive Order ending discrimination on the basis of sexual orientation in determining who may serve in the Armed Forces of the United States." Congress held a series of hearings on the matter in the spring of 1993. While the issue was being debated, the Clinton Administration established an interim policy that prevented military officials from asking recruits about their sexual orientation and placed those in the process of discharge on stand-by reserve.

The final policy, termed "don't ask, don't tell, don't pursue," was intended to be a compromise that would ease restrictions against homosexual service members without leading to an outright removal of the ban. The military would be prohibited from asking a service member about his or her sexual orientation, but it would still be able to discharge service personnel on the basis of credible investigative information, or if the service members voluntarily admitted his or her orientation. Unlike the old policy, which expressly prohibited both homosexual conduct and homosexual status, the new policy was supposed to distinguish between homosexual orientation, which would not be a bar to service, and homosexual conduct, which would be. In February 1994, the Department of Defense issued its directive implementing the new policy. The Department of Defense declared, "A person's sexual orientation is considered a personal and private matter and is not a bar to service unless manifested by homosexual conduct." The directive also stated:

> The Department of Defense has long held that, as a general rule, homosexuality is incompatible with military service because it interferes with the factors critical to combat effectiveness, including unit morale, unit cohesion and individual privacy. Nevertheless, the Department of Defense also recognizes that individuals with a homosexual orientation have served with distinction in the armed services of the United States.
>
> Therefore, it is the policy of the Department of Defense to judge the suitability of persons to serve in the armed forces on the basis of their conduct. Homosexual conduct will be grounds for separation from the military services. Sexual orientation is considered a personal and private matter, and homosexual orientation is not a bar to service entry or continued service unless manifested by homosexual conduct.

By the time that the Department of Defense issued its implementing regulations, however, Congress had already passed legislation that weakened the proposed distinction between conduct and status. On November 30, 1993, the new policy was codified into law by congressional passage of the Defense Authorization Act. The Act reiterates the earlier view that homosexual service members constitute an "unacceptable risk to the high standards of morale, good order and discipline, and unit cohesion." It lists the grounds of discharge as engaging in, attempting to engage in, or soliciting another to engage in homosexual acts; stating one is homosexual or bisexual; or marrying or attempting to marry a member of the same sex. The act emphasizes that homosexual conduct is forbidden at all times, regardless of whether one is off-duty or off base. The legislation also expressly allows for the reinstatement of enlistment questions concerning sexual orientation. Service members may challenge their separation by, among other things, demonstrating that they do "not have a propensity or intent to engage in homosexual acts." Finally, the amendment omits the Clinton Administration's objective of enforcing sodomy laws equally for heterosexuals and homosexuals.

In 1999, the Defense Department issued two policy memoranda clarifying the application of the policy on sexual minorities. The memoranda emphasized that the report of harassment or threats because a service member is perceived to be homosexual do not themselves constitute credible information justifying the initiation of an investigation into the sexual orientation of the member in question. . . .

The prohibition of the service of sexual minorities since the 1940s has not led to their elimination from the U.S. military. Many service members do not know they are homosexual when they enlist; others do not consider themselves to be homosexual, even though their behavior fits the military's strict definition. Some who do identify as sexual minorities join anyway, because they want to serve their country or because of the job opportunities the military provides. Most serve in relative silence, telling only other gay and lesbian service members or a few trusted heterosexual colleagues, if they tell anyone at all. While military investigations have led to the discharges of more than 100,000 service members since the 1940s, experts agree that many more have served without being separated. And as societal attitudes toward homosexuality have in general become more tolerant, there has been increasing evidence of acceptance among many heterosexual military personnel, as well. But the official policy mandates removal of all known homosexual service members, regardless of conduct and regardless of their record. Even those personnel members who experience acceptance from their colleagues remain in danger that a change in command, an unreciprocated advance, or the hostility of one individual could result in the end of their military careers.

Department of Defense officials now acknowledge that many homosexual service members have served honorably and well, and they have discarded the unsupported belief that gays and lesbians are a threat to national security. They do, however, continue to express concern that removing the ban on homosexuality would lead to declines in morale, unit cohesion, and operational effectiveness. In spite of considerable evidence to the contrary from foreign militaries and domestic fire departments, and despite the opinions of social scientists that study group cohesion and interpersonal relations, U.S. military officials continue to deem sexual minorities as inherently threatening to the good working order of the military. The most compelling evidence against such fears comes from what scholars and researchers have learned about the actual service of sexual minorities in the U.S. military. During periods of sustained conflict, when the need for good unit function and operational effectiveness is at its zenith, the numbers of discharges for homosexuality decrease. Further, the policy is not uniformly implemented even in times of peace; some homosexual service members face a lesser chance of discharge than others because of gender, branch of service, or place of duty. Researchers have catalogued scores of examples from the last fifty years of service members who have served openly and with the support and respect of their colleagues.

# Legislation That Limits Gay Rights Is Declared Unconstitutional

SEAN PATRICK O'ROURKE AND LAURA K. LEE DELLINGER

*In the fall of 1992 citizens of the state of Colorado passed a ballot initiative known as Amendment Two. Proposed by a coalition of right-wing organizations, Amendment Two repealed existing protections related to housing, employment, and insurance policies for men and women who are, or who are thought to be, homosexual or bisexual. It also prohibited Colorado citizens from bringing a case of discrimination based on sexual orientation to court. The provisions of the measure were the most sweeping limits to gay and lesbian rights ever proposed in the United States. Researchers Sean Patrick O'Rourke and Laura K. Lee Dellinger explain in this selection how the Colorado Legal Initiatives Project (CLIP) filed the case of* Evans v. Romer *in Denver District Court to contest the law as unconstitutional. CLIP won the decision, but the state of Colorado appealed the case all the way to the U.S. Supreme Court. On May 20, 1996, the Supreme Court also affirmed that Amendment Two violated the equal protection clause of the Fourteenth Amendment to the Constitution. Human rights organizations across the nation applauded the landmark defense of gay rights while some conservative groups condemned it as an attack on American family values.*

Sean Patrick O'Rourke and Laura K. Lee Dellinger, "*Romer v. Evans*: The Centerpiece of the American Gay-Rights Debate," in *Anti–Gay Rights: Assessing Voter Initiatives*, ed. Stephanie L. Witt and Suzanne McCorkle. Westport, CT: Praeger, 1997. Copyright © 1997 by Stephanie L. Witt and Suzanne McCorkle. All rights reserved. Reproduced by permission of Greenwood Publishing Group, Inc., Westport, CT.

"When seven gay-rights activists met on a May afternoon in 1992, sipping weak coffee in a down-at-the-heels conference room on East Colfax Avenue [in Denver, CO], they launched a lawsuit likely to reach the velvet curtained chambers of the U.S. Supreme Court." So wrote Michael Booth, a staff writer for the *Denver Post* newspaper in 1993. Booth was referring to a group of civil rights activists, now known collectively as the Colorado Legal Initiatives Project (CLIP). CLIP had gathered to discuss legal strategy in response to the possible passage of a Colorado anti-gay-rights ballot initiative in the fall of 1992.

## Amendment Two

The initiative, known as Amendment Two because of its place on the ballot, was proposed by Colorado for Family Values (CFV), a right-wing offshoot of the better known Traditional Values Coalition of Anaheim, California. Joining with a cadre of other right-wing organizations (including the Traditional Values Coalition, Focus on Family, Concerned Women for America, Summit Ministries, and The Eagle Forum), CFV filed the initiative petition on July 31, 1991, and the signature drive along with a "no special rights" campaign began. By March 20, 1992 CFV had collected 85,000 signatures, enough to qualify for the Colorado ballot. Activists and legal experts on both sides of the issue agree that, prior to Amendment Two, no measure had ever been attempted in the United States that had as great potential negative impact on the basic civil rights of the gay, lesbian, bisexual community.

CFV proposed Amendment Two largely in response to existing antidiscrimination ordinances in Denver, Boulder, and Aspen, and a proposed ordinance in CFV's base city of Colorado Springs—home to more than eighty conservative groups where more than one third of the 350,000 residents claim to be "born again Christians." The various ordinances CFV sought to invalidate in various Colorado cities quite simply prohibited discrimination based on sexual orientation. The practical effect of the measure was to make it legal and constitutional to discriminate against men and women who are—*or who are thought to be*—homosexual or bisexual, by repealing existing ordinances and policies in Colorado that protect gay men, lesbians, and bisexuals from discrimination in housing, employment, and public accommodation. The measure also prohibited the future passage of antidiscrimination laws protecting homosexuals by state or local government and prevented all governmental bodies from considering any claim of sexual-orientation discrimination. In addition, the amendment would have changed insurance code provisions and invalidated Governor Roy Romer's Executive Order prohibiting discrimination in state employment. But the most far-reaching effect of Amendment Two was to make it impossible, indeed illegal, for government to respond to existing or future discrimination which gay, lesbian, or bisexual Coloradans might encounter by constitutionally prohibiting their right to make a claim.

CFV's prodiscrimination rhetoric had one central theme: "no special rights." Those who fought for the passage of Amendment Two based their campaign on the premise that gay, lesbian, and bisexual Coloradans enjoyed "special rights" because of the ordinances enacted in various Colorado cities. To be successful, they had to convince a public—70 percent of which support equal rights for gay people—that the gay community was, in fact, seeking something *more* than the rest of the citizenry enjoyed. Elizabeth Birch, executive director of the Human Rights Campaign, noted that it was to CFV's advantage "that the majority of Americans do not know that no federal law protects lesbian and gay people from discrimination. Indeed," Birch said, "most people do not know that it is perfectly legal to *fire* someone for being gay in the forty-one states that do not have civil rights protection based on sexual orientation."

CFV's "no special rights" campaign appeared to have succeeded. And on November 4, 1992, six months after

CLIP's first meeting, what many in Colorado's human- and gay-rights communities viewed as their worst nightmare came true, and Colorado became the first state in the nation to pass an anti-gay rights ballot measure. Although the margin of victory was narrow—53.4 percent—the amendment attracted national attention from the anti-gay rights proponents as well as from gay-rights advocates and activists around the nation.

## The Road to the Court

Human-rights activists were confident that Amendment Two was unconstitutional before it ever qualified for the ballot. And as the battle for votes was being waged (and won) by CFV's "no special rights" campaign, CLIP, along with Lambda Legal Defense and Education Fund, the ACLU (American Civil Liberties Union), GLAAD (Gay and Lesbian Alliance Against Defamation), Equality Colorado, and many others were quietly working out the details of their legal strategy.

Nine days after its passage, Amendment Two began the long journey to the U.S. Supreme Court when CLIP filed the case of *Evans v. Romer* in Denver District Court. Just over a month later, the legal team filed a motion for an injunction claiming that Amendment Two was likely to be ruled unconstitutional on the basis of the equal protection clause of the Fourteenth Amendment to the Federal Constitution. The injunction, granted by Judge Jeffrey Bayless on January 15, 1993, kept Amendment Two from being enforced until a trial on its merits could be held. The state appealed the decision, but on July 19, the Colorado Supreme Court upheld the injunction (six to one), affirming the lower court's opinion that equal participation in the political process is a fundamental right and that Amendment Two "fences out" an identifiable group of people from participating in that process. The state of Colorado appealed the decision to the U.S. Supreme Court, which refused to hear the case. Meanwhile, a trial on the merits was held before Judge Bayless in District Court between October 12 and 22,

1993. Two months later, in his December 14 ruling, Judge Bayless found Amendment Two unconstitutional. The ruling was affirmed nearly one year later by the Colorado Supreme Court (six to one). Linda Greenhouse, of the *New York Times*, summarized the Colorado High Court's ruling when she wrote that "any legislation that infringed on the fundamental right to participate equally in the political process by 'fencing out' an independently identifiable class of persons, must be subject to 'strict judicial scrutiny,' meaning the challenged legislation must be shown to be necessary to support a compelling state interest and must be narrowly tailored to meet that interest."

As the legal battle dragged on in Colorado, anti-gay-rights groups across the nation used the Amendment Two victory as impetus for furthering their agenda. And the public was caught in the cross-fire.

Fred Brown, writer for the *Denver Post*, noted in December 1993 that the public seemed to be confused about the effect of Amendment Two. Brown wrote, "throughout the months of debate and public opinion sampling on Amendment Two, it has been clear that Coloradans are convinced they were voting *against* 'special rights' for gays and lesbians, not that they were voting against laws to protect homosexuals from discrimination." Further evidence of public confusion is reflected by research conducted by Talmey Drake Research & Strategies Inc. Their 1993 survey concluded that 71 percent of Coloradans believe that it should be illegal to fire a person based on sexual orientation. Yet Coloradans had just approved a ballot measure that had the practical effect of *making it legal to do just that.* As Amendment Two was making its way through the state courts, citizens in Telluride (February 2, 1993) and Crested Butte (April 5, 1993) passed ordinances *prohibiting discrimination based on sexual orientation.* Obviously, confusion over the effect of Amendment Two was widespread.

[Booth reported that] anti-gay rights activists across the nation continued to make the most of the public confusion by "circulating petitions for anti-gay rights laws in eight states, setting the stage for public votes on proposals ranging from Amendment Two clones to wholesale declarations of public morality." The states of Arizona, Florida, Idaho, Michigan, Nevada, Oregon, and Washington were all engaged in initiative petitioning and "[n]ational political lobbies on both sides of the issue call[ed] 1994 a test year that [would] decide whether the anti-gay movement gains momentum."

In the middle of this divisive battle over citizens rights, activity grew to an all time high in Colorado's gay community. Gay organizations and activities flourished [reported J. Brook of the *Denver Post*,] "including a gay rodeo, gay mountain climbing club and a gay wine tasting club." Ground Zero, a gay-rights organization, published what began as a two-page tabloid covering the Amendment Two battle, then exploded into a twenty-page full-color monthly with more than 1,200 subscribers. In January of 1996 Ground Zero began producing a four-page insert to *The Colorado Springs Independent* newspaper.

As the citizens of Colorado and the nation continued to debate the issue of discrimination against homosexuals, the state of Colorado made its final appeal to the U.S. Supreme Court, which granted *certiorari* [a writ to obtain records of a lower court] on February 21, 1995, and heard argument in October of 1995, just two months shy of the three-year anniversary of the passage of Amendment Two.

## The *Romer* Decision

The Supreme Court handed down its decision in *Romer v. Evans* on May 20, 1996. In a six-to-three ruling, the Court affirmed the ruling of the Colorado Supreme Court and held that Colorado's Amendment Two violated the equal protection clause of the Fourteenth Amendment to the Federal Constitution. The decision, the most significant gay-rights action taken by the Court in ten years, is noteworthy both for its constitutional significance and its passionate rhetoric.

Justice [Anthony] Kennedy began the opinion of the

Court by invoking Justice [John Marshall] Harlan's eloquent dissenting opinion in *Plessy v. Ferguson* (1896). Harlan urged, Kennedy asserted, that the Constitution "neither knows nor tolerates classes among citizens," words that, according to Kennedy, are "now understood to state a commitment to the law's neutrality where the rights of persons are at stake." This principle, enforced by the equal protection clause, required the Court to declare Amendment Two unconstitutional.

## Special Rights

Kennedy's opinion pivots on two central points. At the first he considered Colorado's argument that Amendment Two "puts gays and lesbians in the same position as all other persons," and that the measure "does no more than deny homosexuals special rights."

Kennedy relied upon the "authoritative construction" of the Colorado Supreme Court, which determined that the change in legal status effected by the law was "sweeping and comprehensive." Given this construction, Kennedy reasoned, Colorado's assertion that Amendment Two does no more than deny homosexuals special rights was "implausible." "To the contrary," he wrote,

> the amendment imposes a special disability on those persons alone. Homosexuals are forbidden the safeguards that others enjoy or may seek without constraint. They can obtain specific protection against discrimination only by enlisting the citizenry of Colorado to amend the state constitution or . . . by trying to pass helpful laws of general applicability. This is so no matter how local or discrete the harm, no matter how public or widespread the injury. We find nothing special in the protections Amendment Two withholds. These are protections taken for granted by most people either because they already have them or do not need them; these are protections against exclusion from an almost limitless number of transactions and endeavors that constitute ordinary civic life in a free society.

Far from denying only special rights then, Amendment Two imposed a "special disability" and was therefore held unconstitutional.

## No Rational Basis

The second point around which Kennedy's opinion pivots is the established analysis demanded by "even the ordinary equal protection case." Often called the "rational relation" or "rational basis" test, the inquiry is whether a law that neither burdens a fundamental right nor targets a suspect class bears a rational relation to a legitimate state interest. If so, the law passes constitutional muster.

In *Romer* the Court found that Amendment Two failed the test on two grounds. First, the Court held that the amendment imposed a "broad and undifferentiated disability on a single named group," a targeting of a suspect class that was "at once too narrow and too broad." Because the amendment singled out a specific trait and denied citizens with that trait rights "across the board," it burdened the disadvantaged group far more than the rational relation test could bear. Its reach was not narrowly limited to only what was needed to ensure citizens' freedom of association (Colorado's stated rationale) but rather had the effect of disqualifying an entire class of citizens of the equal protection of the laws.

Amendment Two also failed the test because it raised an inference that the law was the product of an illegitimate state interest. In Kennedy's words, it raised "the inevitable inference that the disadvantage imposed is born of animosity toward the class of persons affected."

The Court concluded that Amendment Two, "in making a general announcement that gays and lesbians shall not have any particular protections from the law" violated the equal protection clause because it inflicted on them "immediate, continuing, and real injuries that outrun and belie any legitimate justifications that may be claimed for it."

The Court's decision did not go unchallenged. Indeed, in

the annals of anti-gay-rights rhetoric, Justice Antonin Scalia's dissenting opinion ranks among the most strident of judicial examples. Scalia took issue with the majority's discussion of Colorado's "special rights" argument and its rational relation analysis. He also disputed the Court's assessment of constitutional precedent and claimed that the decision reached far beyond the judicial realm.

On the special rights argument, Scalia took issue with the majority's reading of the Colorado Supreme Court's interpretation of Amendment Two. He focused on that portion of the earlier opinion that took notice of Colorado laws that proscribed discrimination against persons who are not suspect classes (such as discrimination based on age, marital or family status, and veteran status), and argued that Amendment Two's impact was not as far reaching as the majority asserted. In fact, Scalia argued, Amendment Two did no more than mandate that homosexuals take recourse in the usual, more general political decision making, a mandate that does not abridge the equal protection clause. The majority's claim to the contrary is unsupported by precedent, Scalia argued, "which is why the Court's opinion is so long on emotive utterance and so short on relevant legal citation." Scalia and the dissenters therefore rejected the majority's special rights analysis, and asserted that the people of Colorado had "adopted an entirely reasonable provision which does not even disfavor homosexuals in any substantive sense, but merely denies them preferential treatment."

Similarly, Scalia rejected the Court's rational basis analysis. Relying on the Court's decision in *Bowers v. Hardwick* (1986) upholding Georgia's antisodomy law, Scalia claimed that the long history of legislation criminalizing or otherwise disfavoring homosexual conduct provided an adequate and legitimate rationale for Amendment Two. Indeed, the "moral and social disapprobation of homosexuality" has itself been an important part of the nation's legal history and expression of that view may well be, he implied, a political right.

Finally, Scalia characterized the circumstances that gave rise to Amendment Two as a "culture war," a war best waged in the legislature and other political venues. The Court's "novel and extravagant constitutional doctrine" notwithstanding, the *Romer* decision, in Scalia's opinion "has no foundation in American constitutional law."

## The Reaction to *Romer*

The response to the Court's decision was as divided as the original initiative campaign. While the decision itself was clearly viewed as a victory by Amendment Two opponents, not everyone in the human rights community agreed on the significance. The ACLU, in a statement given by Matthew Cole, director of the group's Lesbian and Gay Rights Project, applauded the High Court's decision saying, "this ruling should bring an end to the anti-gay initiatives that have been proposed in states, cities and towns across the country over the past several years. . . . It establishes as a general principle that lesbians and gay men are entitled to the same constitutional protections granted to everyone else." Elizabeth Birch, the executive director of the Human Rights Campaign, the largest national lesbian- and gay-rights organization, called the ruling "an outstanding moral victory" but said the decision did not advance equal rights for gay and lesbian Americans, rather "[i]t merely ensures that Colorado—and every other state— cannot pass laws to deny gay and lesbian Americans equal access to the democratic process."

Others found the Court's decision wanting. Syndicated columnist James J. Kilpatrick nominated Justice Kennedy's effort the year's "worst opinion from the Supreme Court." Lon Mabon, leader of the Oregon Citizens Alliance, called the decision "an attack on the moral foundation of American culture," and Gary Bauer, president of the conservative Family Research Council, called May 20, 1996, "a very dark day for the liberty rights of the America people."

While the importance of *Romer v. Evans* is evident, the

decision raises at least as many questions as it answers. It seems already to have shifted the debate over gay rights from workplace and public accommodation issues to marriage and personal relations, and it raises questions about the status of existing criminal sanctions against avowedly homosexual conduct. In short, *Romer v. Evans* seems destined to live on as a centerpiece of the American gay-rights debate.

# The Increase in Violence Against Gays Spurs Efforts to Fight Hate Crimes

DAVID M. WERTHEIMER

*The vicious 1998 murder of Matthew Shepard, a gay twenty-one-year-old University of Wyoming student, inspired gays and lesbians to launch a renewed effort to end hate crimes against homosexuals. Activists and organizations had fought against antigay violence since the late 1970s, when several studies revealed the severity and extent of verbal and physical abuse against Americans perceived to be gay or lesbian. The Shepard case garnered unprecedented media attention, which led to increased condemnation of hate crimes based on sexual preference. In the following selection David M. Wertheimer documents early antiviolence efforts and describes the surge in antiviolence activism after Shepard was murdered. Unfortunately, he claims, hate crimes against gays and lesbians have continued to rise as homosexuals' visibility has increased. Wertheimer served as the executive director of the New York City Gay and Lesbian Antiviolence Project from 1985 to 1989. He currently teaches in the Graduate Program in Psychology at Antioch University in Seattle, Washington.*

David M. Wertheimer, "The Emergence of a Gay and Lesbian Antiviolence Movement," in *Creating Change: Sexuality, Public Policy, and Civil Rights*, ed. John D'Emilio, William B. Turner, and Urvashi Vaid. New York: St. Martin's Press, 2000.

In October of 1998, Americans watched in horror as the mainstream media brought the story of Matthew Shepard into virtually every home in the nation. The country seemed shocked that a fragile, twenty-one-year-old University of Wyoming student, targeted because he was gay, would be brutally beaten and left to die tied to a fence post in below-freezing temperatures. Four months later, America watched with renewed horror as the savagely victimized body of Billy Jack Gaither was found in the woods forty miles south of Birmingham, Alabama. Gaither, once again, was targeted by his assailants because of his sexual orientation. These two incidents began to raise the visibility of violence against sexual minorities in a way that no previous incidents had ever been able to accomplish.

Most disturbing, perhaps, is that although these two homicides helped the mainstream media and the American public to "discover" the issue of bias crimes against sexual minorities, these incidents in and of themselves did not in any way represent something new or different. The full extent of anti-gay, -lesbian, -bisexual, and -transgendered violence has, until only recently, gone unrecognized and undocumented. Historically, official reports of hate crimes targeting sexual minorities are virtually nonexistent. Not only have the police and media largely ignored them, but gay, lesbian, bisexual, and transgendered [GLBT] people themselves have been reluctant to come forward subsequent to victimization. Recent research has confirmed what many have suspected for many years—that almost three-quarters of the individuals victimized by antigay and antilesbian violence rarely report the assaults against them to the police. There are many reasons for this underreporting. In addition to facing the shame and pain of the primary victimization suffered at the hands of the initial assailant, sexual-minority crime victims also face multiple layers of "secondary" victimization. This revictimization can include negative responses from family, friends, and traditional social-service agencies. More devastating still, in most parts of the country, where the civil rights of lesbians, gay men, bisexuals, and transgendered individuals are not protected by law, disclosure of an antigay/lesbian assault can lead to the loss of employment, eviction from housing, denial of access to public accommodations, and loss of child custody, all of which can be entirely *legal.* These risks in and of themselves provide an enormous disincentive to the reporting of hate crimes to the authorities. And as the police are willing to tell any crime victim, a crime that isn't reported is a crime that never occurred. . . .

## The Gay and Lesbian Antiviolence Movement

Even as an identifiable crime-victims movement emerged in the United States, it failed to address the nature and extent of hate crimes based on sexual orientation. Grassroots organizing efforts during the late 1960s and 1970s, mostly within women's organizations concerned about violence against women (without specifically identifying the needs of lesbians), gave rise to community-based programs offering a modest range of services to heterosexual, female survivors of domestic violence and sexual assault. Several state governments also initiated the earliest crime-victim compensation programs during this time, and after 1975, municipalities around the country began to fund programs providing crisis-intervention services to a variety of crime victims. Labeled "comprehensive," these programs were often affiliated with municipal or county agencies such as local police departments and district attorneys. The federal government added its own voice to the growing expression of concern for the welfare of crime victims when the Justice Department established its Office for Victims of Crime in 1981. The Presidential Task Force on Victims of Crime studied the problem nationally, issuing its final report in 1982.

And yet, despite these advances during the 1970s and 1980s, many crime-victim populations remained significantly unacknowledged and underserved throughout the

United States. More often than not, crime victims are members of groups that have historically been among the most vulnerable in our society—women, persons of color, children, the elderly, persons with disabilities—populations whose disenfranchisement has resulted in, among other things, a minimizing of the concerns and needs that have traditionally been addressed through social service agencies. Lesbians and gay men are among these vulnerable and disenfranchised subsets of the general population. Although the data that emerged during the 1980s presented a powerful statistical argument, existing crime-victim service networks largely failed to acknowledge or address the existence and needs of lesbian and gay victims of violent crimes. As a consequence of this and other manifestations of systemic heterosexism, lesbians and gay men continued to suffer the often devastating consequences of victimization in isolation and silence. This systemic failure only compounded the initial physical and psychological injuries that follow any bias-related assault.

## Grassroots Antiviolence Programs

Although today [in 1998] more than twenty-five gay, lesbian, bisexual, and transgender-specific antiviolence organizations throughout the United States are organized into the National Coalition of Anti-Violence Programs [NCAVP], the first local antiviolence efforts for sexual minorities in the United States were not organized until almost a decade after the Stonewall riots. The origins of Community United Against Violence (CUAV) in San Francisco, the nation's first successful community organization responding to anti-gay/lesbian hate crimes, may be traced back to the late 1970s when neighborhood "butterfly brigades" were organized, equipping lesbians and gay men with whistles to alert others on the street to bias-related attacks in progress. These concerned citizens responding to local incidents of antigay violence became the foundation of the more organized efforts that followed the massive protests after the assassinations of Mayor George Moscone and openly gay Supervisor Harvey Milk in 1978. By 1979, CUAV had begun to emerge as a structured organization. CUAV was followed in 1980 on the East Coast by the Chelsea Anti-Crime Task Force, later to become the New York City Gay and Lesbian Anti-Violence Project (AVP).

The emergence of the New York City Gay and Lesbian Anti-Violence Project, which in 1998 is the largest program of its type in the nation, is illustrative of how local sexual-minority communities began to identify and respond to the nature of the problem of bias-related violence. Between 1980 and 1990, AVP evolved from a grassroots, neighborhood-specific community network into an agency that is a formally acknowledged member of the larger social-service and crime-victim-service-provider communities. . . .

## The Official Response

Despite the statistical evidence provided by researchers in numerous American cities and the data generated by programs like the New York City Gay and Lesbian Anti-Violence Project and Community United Against Violence, the official response to antigay and antilesbian violence remained minimal. Although several larger police jurisdictions began in the early 1980s to classify and respond to bias crimes based on race, religion, or ethnicity, in New York City the police department's Bias Investigations Unit did not add sexual orientation to its bias categories until July of 1986. Even then, in 1986 the Bias Unit only classified eleven reports as antigay and antilesbian, despite more than 450 cases documented by the AVP.

Even as the gulf remained enormous between community-based organizations documenting the problem of anti-gay/lesbian violence and the timid response of local law enforcement authorities, the momentum behind the gay and lesbian antiviolence movement began to build at the national level. Emerging local community education efforts and victim-service programs joined forces with the

NGLTF's [National Gay and Lesbian Task Force's] Anti-Violence Project to create a national antiviolence presence and agenda. Horrifying personal accounts of bashings publicized in the emerging gay media, combined with local data from fledgling antiviolence organizations, were used by our community's national organizations to force the issue of antigay and antilesbian violence into more mainstream forums. Largely as a result of lobbying done by the American Psychological Association and the NGLTF, Representative John Conyers (D-MI), a member of the House Judiciary Committee, agreed in 1986 to sponsor hearings on antigay and antilesbian violence by the Judiciary Committee's Criminal Justice Subcommittee, which he chaired.

October 9, 1986, was a remarkable day in Congress. The hearing participants included Dr. Gregory Herek from the American Psychological Association, Kevin Berrill from the NGLTF, Joyce Hunter from the Institute for the Protection of Lesbian and Gay Youth (later to become the Hetrick-Martin Institute), Diana Christensen from CUAV, Jacqueline Schafer from the New York County District Attorney's Office, anti-gay/lesbian assault survivors Ed Hassell, Robert Gravel, and Kathleen Sarris, and myself. Members of Congress sat in stunned silence as Washington resident and assault survivor Ed Hassell, sitting in front of the most powerful legislators in the land, offered the following testimony:

> [My assailants] . . . forced me at knifepoint to strip. They beat me. One of them stood on my wrists, leaning over my face, holding the knifepoint at my throat so that any way I moved, it would dislodge him and then he would fall into me, forcing the knife through my throat—while the other one systematically beat me in the groin, the side. They made me address them as "sir." They threatened to castrate me; they threatened to emasculate me. They called me "queer," "faggot." One of them urinated on me. They kept me this way for an hour. There's an old Southern expression called playing possum. I kept trying [to feign unconsciousness] but they were hurting me so badly I couldn't help but to cry out in pain.

Indianapolis lesbian activist Kathleen Sarris offered a similarly chilling account of what happened to her one night as she was leaving and locking up her office. Feeling a gun at the back of her head, she was forced back into the office. Sarris testified:

> For the next three and a half hours. I was beaten, I was assaulted sexually, and I was raped. Throughout the incident, the man kept saying over and over again that the reason he was doing it was to put an end to what was happening [gay rights efforts] in Indiana, and that somebody had to stop the gays and lesbians, and that he, in essence, was going to either kill me or I would walk out of there heterosexual.

NGLTF's Kevin Berrill charged during his testimony that the federal government in general, and the Justice Department in particular, had acknowledged that antigay violence was a major problem but had resisted any efforts to address the issue. Representative Conyers agreed: "Local law enforcement responses to antigay violence have been terrible. Some areas are trying to do a better job than others. Most areas, however, appear to treat the issue as insignificant or somebody else's problem." Berrill presented a set of recommendations on how government could improve its response to antigay and antilesbian violence. These recommendations included:

- Repeal of sodomy laws.
- Passage of local, state, and federal legislation to prohibit gay-related discrimination.
- Passage of legislation to combat antigay violence.
- Establishment of research, education, and programs to monitor anti-gay violence.

Representative Barney Frank (D-MA), who attended the hearings, called the hearings "an important step forward," adding that "you all deserve better from the system, but your willingness to come forward may help us minimize the number of other people who are victimized."

The national exposure for the issue of bias-related violence against sexual minorities that was generated by these congressional hearings was remarkable. Until this time the mainstream media had not significantly covered this issue, which now began to move into the national spotlight. Shortly after the Conyers hearings, a young *New York Times* reporter named William Greer called the New York City Gay and Lesbian Anti-Violence Project and inquired "whether or not there is a story in violence against homosexuals." On November 23, 1986, still during the era in which *The New York Times* identified lesbians and gay men only as "homosexuals," the *Times* ran the first, major mainstream-media article to address the full scope and extent of antigay and antilesbian violence. The story, buried on page 36, almost didn't make it into print at all. Despite the overwhelming evidence provided to the *Times* reporter by researchers and service providers around the nation, the *Times* news editor insisted that the story was not legitimate without corroboration of this data from local and national law enforcement authorities. Yet without official mechanisms for the collection and analysis of hate crimes data involving lesbians and gay men at the local, state, and national levels, such corroboration was impossible. The statistics and case studies cited by representatives of the gay community were considered, by the editor, to represent the subjective political agenda of community activists rather than hard news. Only after heated conversations between the reporter and the editor did the *Times* relent and run the article, but not without a headline that undercut the force of the story itself: "Violence Against Homosexuals Rising," said the first line of the three-column article, with a second headline stating, "Groups Seeking Wider Protection Say."

With *The New York Times* providing the groundwork of an "establishing story" on the topic of anti-gay/lesbian violence, mainstream media coverage of the topic began to increase rapidly. Newspapers throughout the nation began to report on the issue, and the topic became briefly popular on daytime television talk shows such as *Donahue, Oprah,* and *Sally Jessy Raphael.* This visibility not only stimulated a larger public dialogue on antigay violence, but also had a substantial impact on the lesbian and gay communities, particularly in areas outside of New York and San Francisco. . . .

## Media Coverage Leads to Changes in New York

In the wake of the 1986 racially motivated slaying of a young African-American man in the Howard Beach neighborhood of Queens in New York City, Governor Mario Cuomo convened the New York State Governor's Task Force on Bias-Related Violence in 1987. This task force was charged with studying the problem of bias-related violence in New York State through research, analysis, and public hearings and with making recommendations on a broad range of strategies to reduce the incidence of hate crimes throughout the state. As executive director of the New York City Gay and Lesbian Anti-Violence Project, I was one of fifteen members named to the task force by the governor. In its 315-page report, issued in March 1988, the task force issued dozens of recommendations on legislation, education, law enforcement, social services, housing, and the media. After careful deliberation, the task force decided against including specific chapters in its report on bias-related violence against different communities. Rather, hate crimes were considered a class of crimes that have the potential to victimize any person who is or is perceived to be a member of any oppressed community. Sexual-minority concerns were not separated and ghettoized into a separate chapter that any reader could choose to skip over; instead, the issue of antigay and antilesbian violence was sewn into the fabric of each chapter of the report. No one could come away from reading the report without realizing that, when the State of New York referred to bias-related violence, lesbians and gay men were part of the issue. In echoing the wisdom of [lesbian poet] Audre Lorde, the task force report stated:

> The secrecy, isolation, and fear of discovery plaguing

some gay and lesbian victims have an analogue in the experiences of other victims of bias crimes. The horror of reliving the Holocaust strikes the victim of anti-Semitism. The deep historical roots of slavery and oppression and racist rejection of full citizen status aggravate the pain for Black victims. Hispanic and Asian victims struggle with language barriers, scapegoating that degrades the meaning of success, and a threatened sense of belonging. There are many other pains, some shared by all bias crime victims, others primarily affecting one victim group. There is no hierarchy of pain and suffering. All who suffer deserve full recognition and the best care available.

When, in February of 1990, the U.S. Congress considered the legislation that was to become the Hate Crime Statistics Act, the list of organizations and groups that articulated their support for the inclusion of sexual orientation in this bill was impressive. More than ninety national organizations endorsed the legislation, including the American-Arab Anti-Discrimination Committee, the American Baptist Church, the American Jewish Congress, the NAACP [National Association for the Advancement of Colored People], the AFL-CIO [labor organization], the National Council of La Raza, the National Urban League, and many others. In the face of such support, even the lengthy rantings of Jesse Helms (R-NC) went virtually unnoticed when he called the bill "the flagship of the homosexual, lesbian legislative agenda." When this legislation was passed and signed by President George Bush, it became the first law in the nation to specifically identify the needs and rights of lesbians and gay men in any positive fashion.

## Documenting Hate Crimes

Since 1990, incidents of violence against lesbian, gay, bisexual, transgendered, and HIV-positive persons have shown no signs of abating. Documenting the nature and extent of the problem of bias-related violence targeting sexual minorities has been greatly facilitated during the 1990s by the emergence of the National Coalition of Anti-Violence Projects (NCAVP). The model gay and lesbian antiviolence programs developed by larger gay communities in cities such as San Francisco and New York laid the groundwork for replication of these efforts in cities throughout the country. During the late 1980s, organizations documenting incidents of anti-gay, -lesbian, -bisexual, and -transgender violence emerged in such cities as Chicago, Boston, Philadelphia, and Los Angeles. By the late 1990s, organizations documenting incidents of antigay violence and in many cases providing services to survivors of these attacks had emerged in some two dozen cities throughout the nation. Utilizing a uniform data-reporting instrument, the national coalition today provides a vital infrastructure within the sexual-minority community that documents and reports annually on changes in patterns and trends of anti-gay, -lesbian, -bisexual, and -transgender violence.

In 1997, the National Coalition of Anti-Violence Programs documented a total of 2,445 anti-gay, -lesbian, -bisexual, -transgender, and HIV-related incidents in fourteen different jurisdictions throughout the country. Even as the Department of Justice reported that violent crime rates fell dramatically across the country during 1997, reported bias crimes against sexual minorities continued to climb. Perhaps this is not surprising. The more visible our community becomes, the more those who fear or hate us will use violence to render us invisible. Additionally, the increasing visibility of the gay, lesbian, bisexual, and transgender antiviolence movement has stimulated increased community awareness of violence and may be resulting in more reporting of the incidents that do occur. According to the NCAVP, the number of attacks against lesbians and gay men peaks each year in June. June, when most GLBT pride events are held throughout the nation, is the community's month of greatest visibility—and the greatest threat to those who seek to keep sexual minorities powerless in the closet. Nor are the attacks against individuals becoming any less violent. In 1997, 274 incidents nationally involved an assault with a weapon. Seventy of these incidents involved bats, clubs, or blunt objects. Eighty-eight of these incidents involved firearms or knives. Minor injuries were sustained by 505 individuals; 243 individuals reported serious injuries. There were eighteen homicides.

Recent data related to sexual-minority youth may be less dramatic but are equally alarming. In the "1995 Teen Health Risk Survey" of more than seven thousand students conducted by the Seattle, Washington, public school district, 34 percent of 360 students who self-identified as gay, lesbian, and bisexual reported that they had been the target of offensive comments or attacks based on their perceived sexual orientation either at school or on the way to and from school. This compares to a rate of only 6 percent for similar harassment or assault for heterosexual students. The intolerance and lack of acceptance communicated by these hostile acts also appears to have caused suicidal thoughts and behaviors among sexual minority students. A disturbing 36 percent of gay, lesbian, or bisexual students had seriously considered suicide (as compared to 17 percent of the heterosexual students), and 21 percent had actually made a suicide attempt (as compared to 7 percent of the heterosexual students).

## Support and Growth

Fortunately, the increased visibility of the issue of bias-related violence targeting sexual minorities has led to growth among those organizations providing crime-victim services, criminal-justice-system advocacy, and community education. The New York City Gay and Lesbian Anti-Violence Project, for example, has grown from a struggling organization of one and a half staff in 1985 to a vibrant social service agency with more than a dozen staff members. Direct services are funded through a variety of public and private grants and a strong community donor base. Many private foundations, such as the Joyce Mertz-Gilmore Foundation and the Open Society Institute, made their first gay-funding grants to lesbian and gay antiviolence organizations precisely because these groups are less controversial. These and other foundations have sustained and expanded their support of the sexual minority antiviolence movement.

The increasing levels of support have enabled lesbian and gay victim-assistance organizations to expand the scope of their activities outside the arena of bias-related violence. For example, in 1986, New York's AVP was awarded the first grant from a state public health department to develop services for lesbian and gay survivors of domestic violence. In 1987, AVP received funds to develop services for male survivors of sexual assault. In 1990, AVP became the first program in the nation to receive funding to develop an HIV-related violence program. Resources for the innovative services offered by this program were provided by the New York State Health Department, the New York City AIDS Fund, and the New York Community Trust. In addition to these specialized grants, antiviolence organizations around the nation have also secured resources to strengthen organizational infrastructures. For example, standardized data systems are now able to record and monitor incidents of bias-related violence throughout the nation.

As the inclusiveness of the sexual-minority community has expanded, so has the work of our antiviolence programs. Since 1995, the National Coalition of Anti-Violence Programs has been the first and only national group to collect and report data on violence against transgender persons. In 1997, 102 (3.5%) of the victims reporting to the NCAVP self-identified as transgendered persons. The antiviolence movement has also continued to build stronger bridges to the law enforcement community. Sexual-minority community relationships with the police have expanded from the fragile police/gay community rap sessions held by the AVP and the CUAV in the early 1980s. For example, during 1997, the National Coalition of Anti-Violence Programs worked closely with the Federal Bureau of Investigation and played a leading role in the effort to warn gay communities throughout the nation about the activities of spree killer Andrew Cunanan. Many municipal police departments now actively recruit new officers from the sexual-minority community.

## Continuing Struggles

Finally, despite an increasingly conservative atmosphere in local and national legislative bodies, community activism and the broad base of support for antiviolence efforts have kept various legislative initiatives on bias-related violence alive and well. In June of 1998, Senator Edward Kennedy (D-MA) introduced the Hate Crimes Prevention Act of 1998. Under the terms of this bill, it would be a federal crime to harm or attempt to harm someone on the basis of race, color, religion, national origin, gender, sexual orientation, or disability. Offenders could face up to ten years in prison, or life imprisonment if the crime involves kidnapping, aggravated sexual abuse, or murder.

These bills continue to face extensive and powerful opposition. Subsequent to the 1998 murder of Matthew Shepard in Wyoming, several bills were introduced into the Wyoming State legislature to create enhanced penalties for hate crimes committed against individuals because of their race, religion, disability, sexual orientation, national origin, or ancestry. Due to strong opposition to including sexual orientation in this statute, the bill failed to pass a Senate committee. Even a watered-down version of this bill enhancing penalties for bias-motivated crimes committed because of an individual's "membership in a group" failed to win enough votes to pass. In Texas, a statewide hate crimes statute was scuttled in early 1999 so that Republican Texas governor and presidential contender George W. Bush would not have to sign or veto a bill that might be interpreted as being friendly to the gay, lesbian, bisexual, and transgender community. Even after witnessing the bloodied bodies of Matthew Shepard and Billy Jack Gaither, America still resists efforts to call this most extreme form of bigotry by its true name.

Although the struggle is clearly far from over, during the past fifteen years hate crimes targeting lesbian, gay, bisexual, transgendered, and HIV-infected persons have moved from being considered the predictable and accepted consequences of a deviant lifestyle to a legitimate minority-community issue that engenders the outrage of many individuals and organizations throughout the United States.

Rather than suffering in invisibility and silence, victims of bias-related attacks are increasingly able to access the services and supports that promote recovery. By working to care for their own wounded while building bridges to other constituencies that understand the nature and impact of crimes motivated by hatred, the lesbian, gay, bisexual, and transgendered communities have further insured their presence at the table of those who seek to guarantee our basic rights to life, liberty, and the pursuit of happiness.

# The Overturning of a Texas Sodomy Law Provokes Hope and Despair

NANCY GIBBS

*On July 3, 2003, gay rights activists celebrated a major victory when the U.S. Supreme Court ruled against a Texas antisodomy statute. The case dated back to 1998, when John Geddes Lawrence and Tyron Garner were arrested after police officers found them in bed together. As* Time *magazine reporter Nancy Gibbs explains in the following selection, the case extended privacy as a constitutional right to homosexual couples.* Lawrence v. Texas *succeeded where other cases, such as* Bowers v. Hardwick *in 1989, had historically failed to protect gays and lesbians. Opponents of the decision argued that condoning private gay sexual relations undermines America's moral foundation.*

It's not often you hear Supreme Court Justices treat their brethren with such scorn, or trash a recent decision as being dead wrong—or see lawyers weep as a ruling is read. But Thursday [July 3, 2003] was an emotional day inside and outside the court, as preachers prayed and scholars marveled and gay-rights activists struggled to find the right words, since they were more used to slamming the court than saluting it.

Only 17 years ago, the court upheld Georgia's sodomy law in *Bowers v. Hardwick;* but last week the court dumped its own precedent, voting 6 to 3 to throw out a Texas law prohibiting private homosexual conduct. The Texas case arose in 1998 when a neighbor with a grudge called the Houston police to investigate what he claimed was a disturbance next door; the cops arrived to find John Geddes Lawrence and Tyron Garner in bed together and arrested them under Texas' antisodomy laws. The men were each fined $200 and spent the night in jail. Once the Supreme Court agreed to hear the case, hopes rose among gay activists that maybe some of the Justices were ready to reconsider how far the right to privacy extends.

*Lawrence v. Texas* turns an issue that states have historically decided for themselves into a basic constitutional tenet. Even supporters expressed surprise at Justice Anthony Kennedy's language, given this court's allergy to broad social pronouncements. "The petitioners are entitled to respect for their private lives," Kennedy argued. "The State cannot demean their existence or control their destiny by making their private sexual conduct a crime." The court's majority based its landmark decision on a belief in "a realm of personal liberty which the government may not enter." To opponents, it meant that any law based mainly on moral norms was now vulnerable; to supporters, it meant that the court had recognized the legitimacy of homosexual relations, so any law that discriminates against gays could be ripe for reversal. And with that, the latest battle over liberty, morality and privacy begins.

Gay-rights activists declared *Lawrence* a victory on the scale of the *Brown v. Board of Education* decision, which desegregated schools in 1954. Cooler heads noted that in immediate, practical terms the ruling will have nothing like the impact of *Brown*, which fundamentally changed how American families live and learn. Only 13 states still have sodomy laws on their books, and they are seldom enforced.

But in cases like this the symbolism, over time, can

shape the substance, and so there were people on both sides eager to rally their supporters by declaring the ruling a watershed. Even if the sodomy laws weren't often enforced, says Harvard law professor Laurence Tribe, who lost the *Bowers* case and was present in court last week [July 3, 2003], "the existence of these laws was an excuse for harassment and discrimination, and a labeling of a whole group of people for whom this is the primary form of physical sexual intimacy as deviant and criminal. A lot of people feel that that yoke has been lifted."

But opponents felt just as passionately that America's moral foundation was crumbling completely. "The *Lawrence* decision is an error of biblical proportions," says Scott Lively of the Pro-Family Law Center in Sacramento, Calif. "[As a result] I predict the already enormously powerful gay political lobby in our state will consolidate its power further, and that every item on its agenda is going to get pushed through." The dissenters on the high court, led by Justice Antonin Scalia, charged that the majority grounded its decision not in the Constitution or the law but in the climate of the times. By inventing a brand-new constitutional right, they were ignoring the right of citizens in a democracy to pass laws that reflect their values without having courts overrule them. "It is clear from this that the Court has taken sides in the culture war," he wrote in an especially scalding dissent and warned of undermining laws against bestiality, bigamy, prostitution and incest. He further suggested that the court's attempt to cordon off this decision from others, especially gay marriage, was naive.

The decision was not, strictly speaking, a "liberal" one, another sign of a left-tilting court, which earlier in the week upheld the basic principle of affirmative action. Many conservatives of a libertarian streak abhor the idea of a government so vast and intrusive that it tells people what they can do in private.

Still, those who applauded last week's ruling for "confirming the dignity" of homosexuals were setting the bar rather low, given the barriers that remain. "It's one thing to say there's a fundamental right to sexual intimacy," observes Harvard law professor Richard Fallon, "and another to say there's a fundamental right to marriage." Vermont's civil-unions law is still a kind of "separate but equal" equivocation; the military's "Don't ask, don't tell" policy instituted in 1993 has not stopped 9,000 service members from being discharged since then. And in most states, gays do not enjoy the same protection from employment discrimination that others do. Even as he welcomed "the homosexual emancipation," David Smith of the Human Rights Campaign lamented that "you can still be fired from your job for being gay."

Thus the activists' notion that gay marriage is an inevitable outcome of the ruling may be little more than wishful thinking. "When people say the decision means a lot," says Mary Coombs of the University of Miami law school, "what they're doing is not so much saying what it means but what they are going to argue it means. Part of what this will do is energize both the gay-rights movement and the Christian Fundamentalist right."

**CHAPTER 4**

# Debates over Gay and Lesbian Families

# Chapter Preface

In the 1990s the gay rights movement was characterized by a greater attention to diversity. Although bisexuals and transgendered people had always participated in gay activism, their efforts had often been ignored or criticized by mainstream gay and lesbian activists. By the early 1990s bisexuals called for official inclusion in gay pride marches and founded the first national bisexual conference. Similarly, transgendered activists formed groups like Transgender Nation and GenderPAC to call attention to their contributions to the gay rights movement and to lobby for more legal protections for transsexuals and cross-dressers. Increasingly, gay rights events and organizations used the acronym LGBT to include lesbian, gay, bisexual, and transgender people.

The growth and increased visibility of lesbian, gay, bisexual, and transgendered activism after 1990 yielded important gains. In 1993 the Defense Department, at President Bill Clinton's order, changed the ban on homosexuals in the military to a ban on homosexual activity. Media coverage of several brutal attacks on LGBT people prompted increased awareness of antigay violence and hate crimes. Although Colorado became the first state to nullify existing civil rights protections for homosexuals by amending its constitution in 1990, the provision was struck down by the U.S. Supreme Court in 1996. Later, in 2003, the Supreme Court overturned all state antisodomy laws. At a local level, many laws were passed to protect homosexuals from discrimination. Perhaps the greatest gains were made in the area of gay and lesbian unions. In the late 1990s and early 2000s, states such as California, Vermont, and Massachusetts adopted various degrees of legal protection for same-sex couples.

Along with these victories, however, the gay rights movement suffered defeats as well. The religious right led an effort against gay rights during the 1990s and into the new millennium. Several states in America passed versions of the 1996 national Defense of Marriage Act to limit recognition of same-sex marriages. Other states defeated ordinances that protected gay interests in housing, adoption, and employment.

Overall, the era was marked by many achievements, both for the gay rights movement and those opposed to the movement's goals. As both groups struggle to achieve political successes, it is clear that the battle between them will continue well into the future.

# The Religious Right and Gay Activists Spar over Gay Parenting

NANCY D. POLIKOFF

*Up until the mid–twentieth century, family law in the United States consistently disfavored gay and lesbian parents in custody battles. Individuals had little power to actively oppose this trend until the early 1970s, when verdicts in a few court cases challenged the traditional prejudice against homosexual parents. Eventually, organizations like the Lesbian Mothers National Defense Fund (LMNDF), the Lambda Legal Defense and Education Fund, and the American Civil Liberties Union (ACLU) formed a network of lawyers and legal resources to change laws and policies that restricted the rights of gay parents. By the end of the 1970s, however, a growing group of religious conservatives organized to stop gay rights activists from achieving legal parity that included the right to parent a child. Thus the 1980s marked a time of heated battles between gay rights advocates and the Christian right. Many of the struggles focused on custody, adoption, and foster parenting. In this selection attorney Nancy D. Polikoff describes the major court cases concerning the cultural brawls over gay parenting throughout the 1980s.*

Nancy D. Polikoff, "Raising Children: Lesbian and Gay Parents Face the Public and the Courts," in *Creating Change: Sexuality, Public Policy, and Civil Rights*, ed. John D'Emilio, William B. Turner, and Urvashi Vaid. New York: St. Martin's Press, 2000.

S hortly after Ronald Reagan was elected president in 1980, the first national campaign in which the Christian right was a significant force, two conservative senators, Paul Laxalt of Nevada and Roger Jepsen of Iowa, introduced into Congress the Family Protection Act, the right wing's blueprint for a conservative family agenda. Among other things, it would have required withdrawal of federal funds from any entity involved in "advocating, promoting, or suggesting homosexuality, male or female, as a lifestyle," and it would have forbidden the use of Legal Services Corporation funds for any litigation involving "homosexual rights." In his speech before the Senate as he introduced the bill, Senator Jepsen warned that the move to a broader definition of family, which his legislation sought to combat, would lead to the ability of "homosexuals and lesbian couples to adopt children."

In the early eighties, even as the influence of the Christian right grew, the openness and pride of lesbian and gay families also grew. By the mid-1980s, increased media attention widened the exposure of planned lesbian and gay parenting, creating possibilities for lesbians and gay men around the country. In 1982, the Oakland, California, Feminist Women's Health Center opened a sperm bank that provided frozen semen and shipped it anywhere in the country, without discriminating on the basis of sexual orientation. Two videos were produced, *Choosing Children*, in 1984, and *Alternative Conceptions*, in 1985; *Choosing Children* was reviewed in *The New York Times*. Also in 1985, the first book devoted to helping lesbians decide whether and how to become parents was published. Gay newspapers reported numerous regional conferences on choosing children. The National Lesbian Health Care study, conducted in 1985, showed that about one-third of the lesbians studied wanted to become mothers through adoption or alternative insemination. Legal issues for planned lesbian and gay families gained popular attention during this time, as *The New York Times* reported a judge's approval of an adoption by an openly gay man in 1982 and a visitation dispute in 1984 between two women who had raised a child conceived through alternative insemination. By 1985, several legal conferences had addressed the issues caused by this new family form.

## Major Court Battles

Meanwhile, the number of reported cases of custody and visitation disputes between a heterosexual parent and a gay or lesbian parent grew; about twenty states had reported decisions in the first half of the 1980s. New forms of lesbian and gay families confronted the courts for the first time, but the traditional disputes, precipitated when lesbians and gay men came out after they had married and had children, still constituted the greatest number of legal challenges to lesbian and gay parenting. Decisions during this period were no more favorable than those of the 1970s. Some courts eschewed discrimination, such as those in Massachusetts, Alaska, and New York. In 1980, the Massachusetts Supreme Court permitted a lesbian mother to regain custody from a guardian who had cared for her children while the mother was suffering from mental and physical illness. Reversing the trial court decision that would have kept the children with the guardian, the court said that the mother could not lose her children because her household failed to meet "ideals approved by the community" or because she had a lifestyle "at odds with the average." The Alaska Supreme Court ruled in 1985 that a mother's lesbian relationship should be considered only if it negatively affected the child and that it was "impermissible to rely on any real or imagined social stigma attaching to [the] mother's status as a lesbian." A 1984 New York appeals court decision also articulated the requirement of an "adverse effect" before a parent's sexual orientation could be a basis for denying custody, and an appellate case the next year lifted a trial court order prohibiting the presence of the father's partner or any other gay person during visitation.

Most courts, however, ruled against gay parents. Cases from appellate courts in Indiana, North Dakota, South Dakota, and Virginia overturned trial court judges who had awarded custody to lesbian, gay, or bisexual parents. In 1985, the Virginia Supreme Court held that a gay parent living with a partner was always an unfit parent. In Tennessee and Oklahoma, appellate courts affirmed transfers of custody from lesbian mothers to heterosexual fathers. An Ohio trial judge who granted a gay father visitation rights with the restriction that "unrelated" males could not be present during visitation was reversed by an appeals court that found that the judge had not imposed enough restrictions on the gay father. The appeals court, in its 1985 decision, said the state had a "substantial interest in viewing homosexuality as an arrant sexual behavior which threatens the social fabric, and in endeavoring to protect minors from being influenced by those who advocate homosexual lifestyles."

In the early 1980s, Missouri appellate courts issued three opinions against lesbian and gay parents. These would be joined by an additional six in the second half of the 1980s, making Missouri the single worst jurisdiction in the country in which to litigate on behalf of a gay or lesbian parent. A 1980 decision changing custody to a heterosexual father because a lesbian mother permitted her partner to be around her children compared the presence of the mother's partner to the presence of "a habitual criminal, or a child abuser, or a sexual pervert, or a known drug pusher." A 1982 decision affirmed severely limited visitation rights for a gay father, disregarding two expert witnesses who testified, among other things, that there was no reason to fear that the children would be sexually molested by the father or his friends. In spite of the evidence, the court reasoned that "every trial judge, or for that matter every appellate judge, knows that the molestation of minor boys by adult males is not as uncommon as the psychological experts' testimony indicated." Another 1982 decision upheld restrictions on a lesbian mother's visitation, referring to her home as an "unwholesome environment."

## Organizing for Change

As the number of cases grew, it became increasingly important to reach parents and child custody litigators around the country, to arm them with positive precedent from other jurisdictions, and to suggest strategies that held the most likely chance of success. The National Lawyers Guild reprinted its Lesbian and Gay Parent's Legal Guide to Child Custody in 1980 and again in 1985. In 1980, the Lesbian Rights Project published its first annotated bibliography of legal and psychological materials on lesbian mothers and their children. In 1982, the Lesbian Rights Project published the first edition of its Lesbian Mother Litigation Manual. A year later, it published the second edition of its annotated bibliography. In 1985, in conjunction with the National Lawyers Guild, a publisher of legal books for practitioners produced the volume *Sexual Orientation and the Law* with sections on representing gay and lesbian parents. These materials made it possible to transmit more effectively a decade of accumulated experience and wisdom about the legal climate for lesbian and gay parents.

Sustained national attention to the suitability of lesbians and gay men raising children emerged in 1985 in the context of foster parenting. Many states, chronically short of foster homes, licensed lesbian and gay foster parents in the decade from 1975 to 1985, a practice supported by both the American Psychological Association and the National Association of Social Workers. But in May 1985, neighbors of a gay couple in Boston who served as foster parents went to the *Boston Globe* to express their disapproval. The ensuing publicity, in print media and on television, sparked widespread debate about gay men and lesbians raising children. The Massachusetts Department of Social Services removed the children from the home, and the Massachusetts state house voted to prohibit children's placement in lesbian and gay homes, explicitly defining homosexuality as a threat to children's well-being. Although that bill did not become law, Massachusetts changed its policy, issuing regulations that made it almost impossible for lesbians and gay men to become foster parents.

In the wake of that controversy, in 1986 the New Hampshire legislature enacted a law prohibiting adoption, foster parenting, or ownership of a child care facility by lesbians or gay men. Although the child-care-facility provision was struck down as unconstitutional, the bans on adoption and foster parenting were upheld. The state Supreme Court was unwilling to credit the undisputed studies that growing up in a gay or lesbian home would not make a child become gay. Rather, it reasoned that a gay role model might affect a child's sexual orientation, and that this consideration could properly inspire the legislature to prohibit gay and lesbian adoption and foster parenting. New Hampshire became the second state with an adoption ban and the first with a legislatively mandated ban on gay foster parenting. In 1987, President Reagan's Interagency Task Force on Adoption issued its report, which contained a recommendation that "homosexual adoption should not be supported."

As in the past, advocates for gay and lesbian parents continued to represent individual gay and lesbian parents in custody and visitation disputes, hoping to improve the law state by state through appellate court decisions. But during this time they also developed new legal approaches to protect gay and lesbian families in which, from birth, a child had two parents of the same gender. The number of such families continued to grow in the 1980s, and lawyers developed theories using existing adoption statutes in attempts to ensure that both partners would be legally considered the parents of their child.

Lawyers coined the term *second-parent adoption* to describe the equivalent of a stepparent adoption, in which a biological parent's partner adopts her child. The term *joint adoption* was used to designate adoption of a child by both members of a couple, a practice unheard of earlier unless the couple was legally married. The first second-parent adoption was granted in Alaska in 1985, and within months there were others in Oregon, Washington, and California. All these were granted by trial court judges without written opinions, making them of limited precedential value. The adoption decrees were circulated among a small group of legal advocates, who used them to help develop the law in an increasing number of jurisdictions. Although law review articles first discussed these cases in 1986, there was no reported opinion granting a second-parent adoption until 1991.

The mid-1980s also saw the first disputes between separating lesbian mothers who had raised a child together and between a lesbian mother and a semen donor, often a gay man, when disagreements arose about the donor's relationship with the child. These cases would become more prominent in the late 1980s and into the 1990s.

## Bowers v. Hardwick

The U.S. Supreme Court's 1986 decision in *Bowers v. Hardwick* upheld the constitutionality of a Georgia statute prohibiting sodomy between two consenting adults of the same gender. The decision thus left standing criminal sodomy laws in twenty-four states and the District of Columbia. In some states, these statutes had been used explicitly to justify denials of or restrictions on custody or visitation. A positive decision in *Bowers* would have given advocates in those states a powerful weapon for asserting the rights of gay and lesbian parents. Instead, the Court's decision gave tacit approval to reasoning such as that applied by an Arizona appeals court just a few months after the *Bowers* decision. The court affirmed a trial court's unwillingness to certify a bisexual man as an appropriate adoptive parent, reasoning that Arizona had a criminal sodomy statute, that such a statute was constitutional under *Bowers*, and that "it would be anomalous for the state on the one hand to declare homosexual conduct unlawful and on the other create a parent after that proscribed model, in effect approving that standard, inimical to the natural family, as head of a state-created family." The New Hampshire Supreme Court also cited *Bowers* in upholding the state's legislative ban on gay adoption and foster parenting.

Although *Bowers* gave ammunition to courts inclined to disapprove of lesbian and gay parenting, those courts did not need *Bowers* to rule against a gay or lesbian parent; they had been doing so for more than a decade. Conversely, *Bowers* did not require a court to deny the ability of lesbians and gay men to be good parents. The year after *Bowers* a trial judge in South Carolina, a state with a criminal sodomy statute, awarded custody of a child to her lesbian mother, and the appeals court affirmed because it found, among other things, no evidence that the child's welfare was being adversely affected. Thus, although a victory in *Bowers* might have facilitated a step forward for lesbian and gay parents, the defeat preserved the state-by-state status quo.

In the decade or so between the beginning of organized advocacy on behalf of gay and lesbian parents and the decision in *Bowers*, lesbians changed their outlook on sodomy law reform. In the early 1970s, many lesbians resented and considered irrelevant the early gay rights legal movement's emphasis on eradicating criminal sodomy statutes. By the time of *Bowers*, however, the two issues—the right to parent and the right to sexual privacy—did not seem quite so distinct. Sodomy statutes were sometimes cited in custody and visitation cases. Even if the parent in the case was a gay father, the reasoning of the case denying custody or restricting visitation would apply with equal force to a lesbian mother in a subsequent case. Sodomy law reform thus became connected to advocacy on behalf of lesbian and gay parenting.

## After *Bowers*

Since the second half of the 1980s, advocates for lesbian and gay parents have divided their resources between the issues facing parents with children from prior heterosexual relationships and the issues facing planned lesbian and gay families. Because the former issues had been around for more than a decade, by the late 1980s they were well defined; there was both an extensive body of literature analyzing court decisions and a growing number of studies comparing the mental health of children raised by divorced heterosexual mothers to children raised by divorced lesbian mothers. In 1988, the District of Columbia held the first judicial education program in the nation, mandatory for all trial and appellate court judges, designed to overcome myths and bias about lesbian and gay parents.

These developments did not mean that, nationwide, there were more successes. Appellate court decisions from the late 1980s continued to add up both for and against lesbian and gay parents. In 1986, the Nevada Supreme Court terminated a father's parental rights solely because he underwent a sex change operation. In 1987, the Arkansas Supreme Court awarded sole custody to a heterosexual father, reasoning that it was proper to presume the children would be harmed living with their lesbian mother in an "immoral" environment. Missouri continued its rampage of decisions against lesbian and gay parents, adding six between 1987 and 1989 to the three from earlier in the decade.

Meanwhile, there continued to be some successes. In 1988, a New Mexico appeals court overturned a trial judge's refusal to place a neglected child in the custody of his adult brother who was gay. The court reasoned that a proposed custodian's sexual orientation was not enough to conclude that the person would be unable to provide a child with a proper environment. During this period, decisions in California and Washington overturned restrictions on a gay or lesbian parent's visitation rights. A 1987 Ohio court rejected a heterosexual mother's request that her former husband be denied all overnight visitation. The mother specifically urged, and the court specifically rejected, the following arguments: that overnight visitation would trigger "homosexual tendencies" in the children, that they might contract AIDS, that they would suffer social stigma, and that no proof of adverse impact should be required. While the reasoning of the court was extremely positive, the overnight visitation order prohibited the presence of nonrelated males, which the father did not appeal and the court, therefore, did not address. The case was thus a limited victory.

## Developing a Legal Network

The issues facing couples in planned lesbian and gay families during this time were too new for there to be published resources, such as manuals or law review articles, or even much reported law. Like lesbian-mother custody disputes in the 1970s, the development of legal theories took place among a small group of advocates who disseminated their work. An enormous change since the 1970s, however, made this work of dissemination much easier than it had been a decade earlier. The small, informal networks of the mid-1970s, formed by those who met at Women and the Law or National Lawyers Guild conferences or through word of mouth, and the handful of lawyers associated with fledgling gay legal groups, were enhanced by an extensive and coordinated network encompassing local practicing attorneys, increasing numbers of advocates working for national organizations, and openly gay students and faculty at law schools. The ACLU [the American Civil Liberties Union] added a Lesbian and Gay Rights Project in 1986. The National Lesbian and Gay Law Association (NLGLA) was formed at a meeting held in conjunction with the 1987 March on Washington. It linked both an increasing number of local gay bar associations and individual attorneys who represented lesbian and gay clients. In 1988, NLGLA held its first Lavender Law conference, which included panels addressing both traditional custody and visitation disputes and the issues facing planned gay and lesbian families—access to alternative insemination, surrogacy, and adoption; second-parent adoptions; termination of a coparenting relationship through death or dissolution. It took Lambda Legal Defense and Education Fund ten years, from 1973 to 1983, to hire its first full-time attorney, but by 1989 it had four. By the end of the 1980s, a monthly publication of legal developments affecting lesbians and gay men, entitled *Lesbian/Gay Law Notes* and compiled by New York Law School professor Arthur Leonard, had a national circulation of more than a thousand attorneys and legal groups.

Thus, more attorneys had the resources to assist planned lesbian and gay families. Dozens of second-parent adoptions were granted in Alaska, Oregon, Washington, and California, including one granted in Washington in 1989 over the objection of a guardian ad litem appointed to represent the child; the judge found "overwhelming" evidence that the adoption was in the child's best interests. In a 1989 case, a trial court judge in Broward County, Florida, awarded custody of ten-year-old Kristen Pearlman to Janine Ratcliffe, her nonbiological mother. Janine and her former partner Joanie had decided to raise a child together, and Joanie had conceived through anonymous donor insemination. They raised Kristen together until she was six, when Joanie died and a court awarded custody to Joanie's parents. Janine instituted further custody proceedings four years later, after Kristen's emotional health had deteriorated and the grandparents had terminated all contact between Kristen and Janine. In chambers, the child pleaded with the judge to permit her to live with Janine. The judge found that Kristen continued to view Janine as her primary parent figure, that it would be detrimental to Kristen to continue her separation from Janine, and that there was no evidence Janine's sexual orientation would have any detrimental effect on Kristen.

In 1989, the media discovered planned gay and lesbian families. Articles appeared in *The New York Times, The Wall Street Journal, The Boston Globe*, the *San Francisco Exam-*

*iner, The Washington Post,* and *Newsday.* The *Donahue* show and *20/20* (in a show entitled, "I Have Two Moms") featured lesbian couples raising children. In that year, the first children's book appeared whose central character was a child born of anonymous-donor insemination to a lesbian couple, and its initial printing of four thousand copies sold out before publication. In 1990, at the annual conference of Gay and Lesbian Parents Coalition International (GLPCI), a group of children of lesbian and gay parents held their own series of meetings out of which emerged a national organization called Children of Lesbians and Gays Everywhere (COLAGE). The first generation of children raised by lesbian mothers and gay fathers who came out in the early and mid 1970s had reached adulthood.

## Divorce Issues

Inexorably, the formation of lesbian and gay families with children resulted in the subsequent dissolution of some of those families. Beginning in the late 1980s and continuing throughout the 1990s, these dissolutions have presented courts with two options—recognize planned lesbian and gay families and modify family law principles to protect the interests of parents and children in such families, or maintain a rigid definition of parenthood grounded in a biologically based, heterosexual norm and thereby obliterate the reality of children's lives with their lesbian and gay parents. Courts have usually chosen the latter option. In most states that have faced the issue, courts have refused to look beyond biology or the legal status conferred by formal adoption.

Disputes about parenthood have arisen primarily in two contexts. The first is a claim by a nonbiological parent to continue a relationship with a child when she and the child's biological parent separate. The second is a claim by a biological father, usually a semen donor, who demands legal parental status in disregard of an agreement with the lesbian couple that he would not assert formal parental rights based on biology.

These cases initially posed a dilemma for gay and lesbian legal organizations. The National Center for Lesbian Rights [NCLR], for example, had a policy of not representing one lesbian against another. Yet it became apparent early on that in lesbian breakups the parent with the legal status was using doctrine designed to protect parents from outsiders, such as relatives or temporary child-care providers, for the purpose of excluding from the child's life a former partner who had functioned as the child's parent. Even if the legally unrecognized mother stayed home with the child, or if the child called both women "Mommy," or had the last name of the legally unrecognized mother, or asked to live with, or at least visit, the person s/he clearly considered another parent, courts rejected such claims through a narrow definition of parenthood tied to a heterosexual paradigm of family. Thus NCLR reexamined its policy and determined, as did the other legal organizations, that it would advocate upholding the family deliberately formed by the couple and their children and oppose a legal parent's attempts to write the legally unrecognized parent out of the child's life.

This advocacy has been largely unsuccessful. Appellate courts in California and New York, the states with the largest number of planned lesbian and gay families, have both closed the door on all claims by nonbiological mothers and recognized the claims of semen donors. Claims on behalf of nonbiological mothers have also been rebuffed in Ohio, Texas, and Florida. The measure of the vulnerability of legally unrecognized parents is the celebration engendered by a 1995 Wisconsin Supreme Court decision permitting such parents to request visitation rights, even though the decision also foreclosed any request for custody, even if the nonbiological parent was the child's primary caretaker. In Vermont, the first state whose Supreme Court approved second-parent adoptions, the Supreme Court has also ruled that in the absence of such an adoption, no factual scenario, no matter how compelling, would require a legally recognized parent to continue contact between her child and the child's legally unrecognized parent.

## Legal Dilemmas for Gay Parents

Advocacy for the integrity of planned lesbian and gay families has posed a dilemma for advocates for lesbian and gay parents. Doctrine that makes it difficult for nonparents to obtain custody has historically protected lesbian mothers from claims by their own relatives or relatives of a child's father. A lesbian mother whose former husband does not challenge her for custody is protected from claims by other relatives by doctrine that makes it difficult for a nonparent to challenge the custody rights of a parent. It is precisely this legal doctrine, however, that courts apply to rebuff the claims of a lesbian who has functioned in every way as a child's coparent but who lacks legal status. The distinction between a coparent and, for example, a grandparent could be made in carefully written legislation, but because lesbian and gay advocates cannot use the political process on behalf of lesbian and gay families without incurring political backlash, this avenue had been largely foreclosed. Advocates are left asking courts to walk a fine line between opening the door in true coparenting situations while not opening it so far that more lesbian and gay parents are vulnerable to claims by antigay relatives. Almost all courts have declined this invitation in the absence of legislative guidance, leaving lesbian and gay coparents in the category of all other nonparents and therefore without legal recourse.

# The Debate over Same-Sex Marriage

NOLO LAW FOR ALL

*Same-sex couples in the United States have been attempting to achieve legal recognition for their unions since the early 1970s. In the new millennium marriage has resurfaced as a legal goal for same-sex couples. In this selection NOLO Law for All provides the historical and legal context for contemporary gay marriage debates. As NOLO explains, Massachusetts legalized gay marriage in May 2004, and several cities and counties throughout the United States began to issue marriage licenses to same-sex couples in the absence of any specific laws forbidding gay marriage. Other states, such as Vermont, Hawaii, New Jersey, and California, have passed legislation to provide same-sex couples with some of the traditional marriage benefits and protections without legalizing gay marriage per se. At the same time, opponents of same-sex marriage have proposed a federal constitutional amendment (which to date has not been approved) along with state-by-state measures to ban gay marriage. NOLO Law for All is a publisher of legal information to enable people to handle their own everyday legal matters. The company currently publishes* A Legal Guide for Lesbian and Gay Couples.

A common dictionary definition of family is "the basic unit in society having as its nucleus two or more adults living together and cooperating in the care and rearing of their own or adopted children." Despite this all-

---

inclusive definition, a lesbian or gay couple—with or without children—has not been what many people picture when they think of a family.

Nevertheless, lesbian and gay couples (and their children) do live in families and have sought societal recognition of their families over the past several decades. It began in the early 1970s, when same-sex couples applied for marriage licenses, asked courts to allow one partner to adopt the other, and took other steps to legally cement their relationships. Many of these efforts failed, but some progress was made. By the mid 1980s, same-sex couples were seeking domestic partnership recognition from cities and private companies. This effort continued with increasing strength in the 1990s and on into the new century. In recent years, same-sex couples have made enormous strides toward equal recognition of their families.

## Same-Sex Marriage in U.S. Cities

San Francisco Mayor Gavin Newsom really started something on February 12, 2004, when he ordered city clerks to begin issuing marriage licenses to same-sex couples. Since then numerous other U.S. cities have followed his lead, and the entire country's attention has been drawn to the debate. But it will be a while before the issue is settled. Lawsuits in San Francisco and elsewhere are making their way through the courts[1], and Congress is poised to consider a

---

1. The Human Rights Campaign reports:
    The state supreme court ruled Aug. 12, 2004, that the city of San Francisco did not have the authority to issue marriage licenses to same-sex couples. It also ruled that the 4,037 marriage licenses that had been issued to same-sex couples were void and without any legal effect. The California Supreme Court did not rule on whether California marriage law, which excludes same-sex couples from marrying, violates the California constitution.
    Cases dealing with the constitutional issue are working their way through the trial courts and may be decided by the California Supreme Court at a later date. The National Center for Lesbian Rights, Lambda Legal, and the American Civil Liberties Union filed a lawsuit March 12, 2004, in state court, *Woo v. Lockyer.* The suit, filed on behalf of ten same-sex couples along with the San Francisco–based Our Family Coalition and Equality California, a state GLBT-rights group, challenges Proposition 22. This state law, which defines marriage as between a man and a woman, was championed by the late state senator Pete Knight, R-Palmdale,

constitutional amendment prohibiting same-sex marriage[2]. All of these legal proceedings will take time, so we're unlikely to have a clear decision any time soon. Meanwhile, the legality of the marriages that have been performed is in question, and it's unclear if those marriages will be recognized outside of the city or county where the licenses were issued.

The most promising development in the fight for same-sex marriage is the recent Massachusetts Supreme Court decision in *Goodridge v. Department of Public Health* (November 2003). The court held that the state law barring same-sex marriage was unconstitutional under the Massachusetts constitution and ordered the legislature to remedy the discrimination within six months. In February 2004, the court ruled that offering civil unions instead of civil marriage would not meet the requirements set forth in *Goodridge*. As a result, beginning in May 2004, same-sex couples will be able to get marriage licenses and enter into civil marriages. The Massachusetts legislature is currently considering an amendment to the state constitution to forbid marriage between same-sex couples, but the soonest such an amendment could take effect is 2006.

## Marriage-Like Relationships in Other States

*Vermont: Civil Unions*

In 1999, the Vermont Supreme Court ordered its state

and passed by voters in 2000. San Francisco city attorney Dennis Herrera has also filed a suit challenging the exclusion of same-sex couples from marriage, which was consolidated with *Woo v. Lockyer*. The suit is now proceeding in San Francisco Superior Court.

The Marriage License Non-Discrimination Act (A.B.1967), sponsored by Equality California and introduced in the California Assembly by Assemblyman Mark Leno, D-San Francisco, would overturn Proposition 22, the state law defining marriage as between a man and a woman. On April 20, 2004, the State Assembly Judiciary Committee voted 8 to 3 to send the bill forward, marking the first legislative vote in favor of marriage equality in the United States. On May 18, however, Leno confirmed that the bill would be shelved until the end of the year.

2. U.S. senator Wayne Allard (R-CO) reintroduced the Marriage Protection Amendment (MPA) on the Senate floor in January 2005. The amendment, if passed, would define marriage as solely "the union of a man and a woman."

legislature to come up with a system providing same-sex couples with traditional marriage benefits and protections. (*Baker v. State*, 1999). In response to the supreme court mandate, the Vermont legislature passed the Vermont Civil Union law, which went into effect on July 1, 2000. While this law doesn't legalize same-sex marriages, it does provide gay and lesbian couples with many of the same advantages, including:

- rights under family laws such as annulment, divorce, child custody, child support, alimony, domestic violence, adoption, and property division
- rights to sue for wrongful death, loss of consortium, and under any other tort or law concerning spousal relationships
- medical rights such as hospital visitation, notification, and durable power of attorney
- family leave benefits
- joint state tax filing, and
- property inheritance when one partner dies without a will.

These rights apply only to couples living in Vermont. But even for Vermont residents this new civil union law does not give same-sex couples the rights and benefits federal law provides to male-female married couples. Same-sex couples are not eligible for Social Security benefits, immigration privileges, or the marriage exemption to federal estate tax. Vermont also permits reciprocal beneficiaries relationships which provide the same health care decision-making rights available to spouses and couples in civil unions.

*Hawaii: Reciprocal Beneficiaries*
Hawaii's Reciprocal Beneficiaries law provides some marriage-like benefits. Any two state residents can register as reciprocal beneficiaries, as long as they are over 18 and are not permitted to marry. Couples who sign up gain some of the rights and benefits granted by the state to married couples, including hospital visitation rights, the ability to sue for wrongful death, and property and inheritance rights.

*New Jersey and California: Domestic Partnerships*

New Jersey is the most recent addition to the list of states that offer marriage-like benefits to their citizens. The new domestic partner law, passed in January 2004, applies to same-sex couples and to opposite-sex couples in which one partner is 62 or older. The benefits provided include equality with married couples in insurance coverage and medical decision making and the choice of filing joint state tax returns. However, the law does not provide for inheritance rights, the right to petition for spousal support if the relationship ends, or automatic parental rights—second parents still have to petition for adoption.

In California, the updated domestic partner law gives broad new rights and places extensive new responsibilities on registered partners. As of January 1, 2005, registered domestic partners in California will have many of the same rights and obligations as legally married spouses under state law, including community property rights and the right to receive support from one's partner after a separation. Domestic partners will both be considered legal parents of a child born into the partnership, without the necessity of an adoption. Superior courts will have jurisdiction over termination of domestic partnerships, unless the relationship was of short duration and there are no children and no jointly owned property. There has been significant backlash against the new law, but the opposition has suffered recent setbacks and failed to get enough signatures for a March 2004 ballot referendum that would repeal the law. It's also unclear what legal effect a marriage entered into in San Francisco has on a domestic partnership of the same partners.

## Recognition from State to State

It remains to be seen what effect the laws in California, Hawaii, New Jersey, and Vermont—and same-sex marriages entered into in Massachusetts and in San Francisco and other cities that are issuing marriage licenses—will have on the rest of the nation. Couples that aren't Vermont residents are allowed to register their civil unions in Vermont, but it is doubtful that other states will recognize their status (except New Jersey, where the law explicitly states that it will recognize civil unions and domestic partnerships from other states, and perhaps California and Hawaii). Likewise, California registered domestic partners will probably have trouble having their partnerships recognized anywhere except Hawaii, New Jersey, and Vermont.

Although the U.S. Constitution requires each state to give "full faith and credit" to the laws of other states, the federal Defense of Marriage Act (DOMA), passed in 1996, expressly undercuts the full faith and credit requirement in the case of same-sex marriages. Many states have also passed DOMA laws, specifically barring same-sex marriages in that state. Because of the apparent conflict between the federal DOMA and the U.S. Constitution, as well as all the other uncertainties in this area, equal rights advocates—and their opponents—are eager to have the U.S. Supreme Court decide the issue of same-sex marriage once and for all.

## Court Cases Involving Same-Sex Marriage Attempts

*Baker v. Nelson* (Minnesota, 1971). A gay male couple argued that the absence of sex-specific language in the Minnesota statute was evidence of the legislature's intent to authorize same-sex marriages. The couple also claimed that prohibiting them from marrying was a denial of their due process and equal protection rights under the Constitution. The court stated that it could find no support for these arguments in any United States Supreme Court decision.

*Jones v. Hallahan* (Kentucky, 1973). A lesbian couple argued that denying them a marriage license deprived them of three basic constitutional rights—the right to marry, the right to associate, and the right to freely exercise their religion. The court refused to address the constitutional issues, holding that "the relationship proposed does not authorize the issuance of a marriage license, because what they propose is not a marriage."

*Singer v. Hara* (Washington, 1974). A gay male couple argued that denying them the right to marry violated the state Equal Rights Amendment. The court disagreed, holding that the purpose of the statute was to overcome discriminatory legal treatment between men and women on account of sex.

*Adams v. Howerton* (Colorado, 1975). The couple, a male American citizen and a male Australian citizen, challenged the Board of Immigration Appeals refusal to recognize their marriage for the purpose of the Australian obtaining U.S. residency as the spouse of an American. (The couple participated in a marriage ceremony with a Colorado minister and had been granted a marriage license by the Boulder, Colorado county clerk.) The court ruled that the word "spouse" ordinarily means someone not of the same sex. Then it noted the 1965 amendments to the Immigration Act, which expressly barred persons "afflicted with sexual deviations" (homosexuals) from entry into this country. The court concluded that it was unlikely that Congress intended to permit homosexual marriages for purposes of qualifying as a spouse of a citizen, when the Immigration Act explicitly bars homosexuals from entering into the United States.

*Thorton v. Timmers* (Ohio, 1975). A lesbian couple sought a marriage license. In denying their request that the court order the clerk to issue them a license, the court concluded that "it is the express legislative intent that those persons who may be joined in marriage must be of different sexes."

*De Santo v. Barnsley* (Pennsylvania, 1984). When this couple split up, De Santo sued Barnsley for divorce, claiming that the couple had a common-law marriage. A common-law marriage is one where the partners live together and act as a married couple, without going through a formal marriage ceremony. Only a few states still recognize common-law marriages—in 1984 Pennsylvania was one of those states. The court threw the case out, stating that if the Pennsylvania common-law statute is to be expanded to include same-sex couples, the legislature will have to make that change.

*Matter of Estate of Cooper* (New York, 1990). Cooper died, leaving the bulk of his property to his ex-lover. His current lover sued to inherit as a surviving spouse under New York's inheritance laws. The court concluded that only a lawfully recognized husband or wife qualifies as a surviving spouse and that "persons of the same sex have no constitutional rights to enter into a marriage with each other."

*Dean v. District of Columbia* (Washington, DC, 1995). Two men sued the District of Columbia for the right to get married. They lost their case at the lower level and appealed. They lost again at the appellate level when the court decided, under current D.C. laws, that the district can refuse to grant marriage licenses to same-sex couples.

*Baehr v. Miike* (Hawaii, 1999). A nine-year battle over the issue of same-sex marriages ended just 11 days before the Vermont ruling in *Baker v. State*, discussed below. The plaintiff in the *Baehr* case argued that Hawaii's marriage license rules were discriminatory. The case set off a national debate over same-sex marriage rights and prompted an onslaught of state and federal legislation designed to preempt the possibility that other states would be forced to recognize same-sex marriages from Hawaii. The case was finally dismissed on the grounds that the legislature had passed a prohibition on same-sex marriages before the Hawaii Supreme Court could render a favorable opinion.

*Baker v. State* (Vermont, 1999). Same-sex couples sued the state, the City of Burlington, and two towns, saying that refusal to issue them marriage licenses violated the Vermont Constitution and the state marriage laws. The Vermont Supreme Court, reversing a lower court decision, declared that the constitution required the state to extend to same-sex couples the same benefits and protections provided to opposite-sex couples. In response, the state legis-

# Gay Marriage Becomes a Wedge Issue in American Elections

LISA ANDERSON

*During the 2004 political campaign issues of concern to gays and lesbians in the United States were fiercely debated. In February 2004 Republican president George W. Bush, who was running for reelection, publicly endorsed efforts to pass a federal amendment to limit marriage "to one man and one woman"—a move that would ban same-sex marriage. Shortly after that, Massachusetts, the home state of Bush's Democratic opponent, Senator John Kerry, legalized same-sex marriage on May 17, 2004. After the Massachusetts victory, opponents of legalized gay marriage brought ballot measures forward in eleven states to limit or ban recognition of same-sex relationships. Many polls showed that gay and lesbian issues played a central role in voter decisions. In the following selection* Chicago Tribune *national correspondent Lisa Anderson examines how the gay marriage issue mobilized activists on both sides of the debate to create a strong voter turnout for election day. Republican voters carried both the presidential and congressional races on November 2. The Federal Marriage Amendment failed to pass in Congress, but all eleven states passed their legislation to limit or ban gay marriage.*

they view as writing discrimination into the Constitution.

"Our country has never witnessed anything of this magnitude in terms of an organized drive to take away rights from a minority. Never," said Matt Foreman, executive director of the National Gay and Lesbian Task Force, a political advocacy group that promotes civil rights for gays and lesbians and mobilizes their vote.

"It's obvious to anyone who looks at it that this is inextricably linked to partisan politics," Foreman said of the marriage amendment. "Gay people see through that immediately, and that also energizes them.". . .

The broadest coalition of gay, lesbian, bisexual and transgender groups ever assembled in Dallas-Ft. Worth held a rally against the amendment under the slogan "Defend, Don't Amend." Drawing more than 500 people . . . , the event was sponsored by StandOut!, a group supported by more than 20 organizations ranging from the Dallas Gay and Lesbian Alliance to a gay bowling association.

"Is it the fight of our lifetime? Yes," said Steve Atkinson, 41, a real estate agent, prominent Democrat and gay-rights activist in Dallas who was involved in founding StandOut! and planning the rally.

## "Not Everybody Gets It Yet"

"This is huge. This is huge, huge, huge," said Atkinson's real estate brokerage partner Lory Masters, 57. "And not everybody gets it yet. A lot of people feel it could never happen. But it could."

A lifelong Republican who will not vote for Bush in November, Masters, who also helped found StandOut!, is a veteran activist who has served on nine national boards of gay and lesbian organizations during the past 30 years.

To become part of the Constitution, the Federal Marriage Amendment must be passed by a two-thirds majority in both houses of Congress and approved by 38 states. The measure appears unlikely to pass this year.

Nonetheless, Rev. Michael Piazza, dean of Dallas' Cathedral of Hope, shares Masters' concern that many in the gay community, ambivalent about marriage, are missing the more serious and far-reaching implications of the amendment. His church runs a get-out-the-vote program and plans educational forums on issues surrounding "marriage equality" and the federal amendment.

"It really is about civil rights and discrimination and the danger of putting that into the Constitution for the first time," said Piazza, leader of the largest gay and lesbian church in the world, with about 4,000 members. "All the amendments before have been about an expansion of rights, not a contraction of rights. It would establish a class of people for whom discrimination would be constitutionally acceptable."

Speaking of his partner of 20 years, with whom he is raising two daughters, Piazza said that, as a couple, "We have no, not any, not a single, solitary civil right in Texas."

Should the Federal Marriage Amendment pass, he said, he fears it would roll back rights that homosexuals already have won, such as insurance for same-sex partners, and might result in further discrimination on the state and local levels, such as in the workplace and housing.

"While that would never happen, probably, in New York or Illinois, it probably would happen in Texas or Mississippi in a heartbeat," Piazza said.

## Beyond Party, Ideology

In the gay community, opposition to the marriage amendment has forged a broad bridge over partisan and ideological differences. In 2000, exit polls conducted by the now-defunct Voter News Service reported that of self-identified gay and lesbian voters, 3 million voted for Al Gore and 1 million voted for George W. Bush.

In terms of the GOP making an appeal to the religious right wing, "We have seen this playbook before," said Christopher Barron, political director of the Log Cabin Republicans, which recently launched a $1 million national

TV ad campaign against the amendment. "The president won in 2000, no matter how many evangelicals stayed home," he said during the gay organization's recent convention in Palm Springs, Calif.

Barron referred to the estimated 9 million evangelical Christians who did not vote in 2000 because of their dissatisfaction with the Bush platform and whom the GOP is trying to lure back in 2004.

"Ten years from now, no one, except in a very few places, will be able to run and win without the gay and lesbian vote. We're committed to making sure this party is on the right side of history," Barron said.

"Especially in the presidential race, we'll either elect someone to the office of president who will use that office to promote this amendment or someone like John Kerry, who won't lend this amendment any credence," said John Marble, communications director of the National Stonewall Democrats, the country's largest Democratic organization for gays, lesbians, bisexuals and transgenders. While Kerry, the presumptive Democratic nominee, opposes the amendment, he does not support same-sex marriage.

In terms of mobilizing the gay vote, the Cathedral of Hope's Piazza said, "What we need to do is be as strategic as the religious right has been. The religious right targets precinct by precinct, so state legislatures are radically more conservative than the states themselves."

The National Gay and Lesbian Task Force has adopted such a grass-roots approach, Foreman said, particularly in such battleground states as Ohio, Oregon and Michigan, where conservative groups are gathering signatures to get amendments banning same-sex marriages on the ballot.

"What we're really focusing on now is voter identification. That means going door to door, having face-to-face conversations with voters, determining where they stand on our issues and then getting them out to vote," Foreman said.

In 2002, he said, such a strategy contributed to Miami-Dade County in Florida retaining an ordinance banning discrimination based on sexual orientation. The task force identified 94,000 anti-discrimination voters and got them out to vote, and "it was clear in the result that that was what made the difference," Foreman said.

## Impact in Tight Race

The votes of gays, lesbians and those who support their issues could have an impact in a presidential race expected to be just as tight as the one in 2000, when often a few hundred votes in a state tipped the balance.

"It will make a difference," said Chuck Wolfe, president of the Gay & Lesbian Victory Fund, which trains and encourages gays and lesbians to run for public office on the federal, state and local levels. "It's very hard to throw the kind of bomb into the gay and lesbian community that the president threw and not have people feel the effects," he said, referring to Bush's support of the Federal Marriage Amendment.

"We are feeling it positively," he said, in terms of a record number of openly gay and lesbian people running for Congress. "I am confident that candidates around the country will feel it negatively. You will see a movement away from the Federal Marriage Amendment by November, especially among elected officials."

## 1910

Anarchist Emma Goldman begins to speak in favor of homosexual rights in the United States.

## 1924

The first gay rights group in the United States is established by a Chicago immigrant named Henry Gerber.

## 1933

Nazis in Germany burn the library of Magnus Hirschfeld's Institute for Sexual Research and destroy the institute.

## 1937

Nazis begin to use the pink triangle to mark homosexuals in their concentration camps.

## 1945

Allied forces liberate the Nazi concentration camps, yet those interned for homosexuality are not freed but forced to serve the full term of their sentences. The Veterans Benevolent Association becomes the first gay and lesbian membership-based organization in the United States.

## 1948

Alfred Kinsey publishes *Sexual Behavior in the Human Male*, revealing to the public that homosexuality is far more widespread than commonly believed.

## 1951

The Mattachine Society is formed as a support group and gay rights organization in Los Angeles.

## 1954

Senator Alexander Wiley requires the U.S. postmaster general to block the gay magazine *ONE* from using the mail because of its "advancement of sexual perversion." Mail distribution of *ONE* is prevented until the decision is overruled by the Supreme Court in 1958.

## 1955

The lesbian organization Daughters of Bilitis is formed in San Francisco by Del Martin and Phyllis Lyon.

## 1956

The first issue of the lesbian newspaper the *Ladder* is published by the Daughters of Bilitis.

## 1962

Illinois becomes the first state in the United States to remove its antisodomy law from its statute.

## 1967

The word *homophobia* is first used in Wainwright Churchill's *Homosexual Behavior Among Males.*

## 1968

Canada repeals all antisodomy laws.

## 1969

The Stonewall uprising in New York marks the beginning of a militant gay liberation movement.

## 1979

The first gay rights parade is held in New York City.

## 1972

Ann Arbor, Michigan, becomes the first city to pass a gay rights ordinance in the United States.

## 1973
The American Psychological Association removes homosexuality from its *Diagnostic and Statistical Manual–II*.

## 1977
Openly gay politician Harvey Milk is elected as a San Francisco city supervisor. Dade County, Florida, enacts a human rights ordinance protecting gays and lesbians. It is repealed in the same year after an anti–gay rights campaign by Anita Bryant.

## 1978
Harvey Milk is assassinated by fellow San Francisco city supervisor Dan White.

## 1979
The first U.S. gay rights march on Washington, D.C., occurs.

## 1981
The Moral Majority starts an antigay crusade.

## 1982
Wisconsin becomes the first U.S. state to pass a gay civil rights law. The U.S. Centers for Disease Control and Prevention replaces the name GRIDS (Gay-Related Immune Deficiency Syndrome) with AIDS (Acquired Immune Deficiency Syndrome).

## 1988
The first World AIDS Day is held by the World Health Organization.

## 1993
The "don't ask, don't tell" policy is instituted in the U.S. military, permitting gays to serve in the armed forces but forbidding homosexual activity.

# 1996

In *Romer v. Evans* the Supreme Court strikes down Colorado's Amendment Two, a law that denied gays and lesbians protection from discrimination.

# 2000

Vermont's civil union law comes into effect, making it the first state in the United States to provide same-sex couples with rights.

# 2003

Episcopal Church leaders in the United States vote to accept the election of the American Anglican Church's first openly gay bishop, Reverend Gene Robinson. Conservative church members warn the move could cause a split in the church. The U.S. Supreme Court rules in *Lawrence v. Texas* that antisodomy laws in the United States are unconstitutional.

# 2004

San Francisco city officials marry a lesbian couple at city hall, defying a state ballot measure defining marriage as a union between a man and a woman. More than thirty-two hundred same-sex couples are married in the following days. President George W. Bush calls on Congress to prepare a constitutional amendment that would ban same-sex marriage and "define and protect marriage as the union of a man and woman as husband and wife." The California Supreme Court orders San Francisco to stop issuing same-sex marriage licenses. City clerks across Massachusetts hand out marriage licenses to same-sex couples as Massachusetts becomes the first state in the United States to legalize gay marriage.

# Organizations to Contact

**Alliance for Marriage (AFM)**
PO Box 2490, Merrifield, VA 22116
Web site: www.allianceformarriage.org

The Alliance for Marriage is a nonprofit organization dedicated to promoting traditional marriage and addressing fatherless families in the United States. AFM works to prevent gay marriage and to educate the public, the media, elected officials, and civil leaders on the benefits of heterosexual marriage for children, adults, and society.

**American Civil Liberties Union (ACLU) Lesbian and Gay Rights Project**
125 Broad St., New York, NY 10004
(212) 549-2627
Web site: www.aclu.org

The ACLU is the nation's oldest and largest civil liberties organization. Its Lesbian and Gay Rights Project, started in 1986, handles litigation, education, and public-policy work on behalf of gays and lesbians. The union supports same-sex marriage. It publishes the monthly newsletter *Civil Liberties Alert*, the handbook *The Rights of Lesbians and Gay Men*, the briefing paper "Lesbian and Gay Rights," and the books *The Rights of Families: The ACLU Guide to the Rights of Today's Family Members* and *Making Schools Safe: An Anti-harassment Training Program for Schools.*

**Canadian Lesbian and Gay Archives**
Box 639, Station A, Toronto, ON M5W 1G2 Canada
(416) 777-2755
Web site: www.clga.ca

The archives collects and maintains information and materials relating to the gay and lesbian rights movement in Canada and elsewhere. Its collection of records and other materials documenting the stories of lesbians and gay men and their organizations in Canada is available to the public for the purpose of education and research. It has published numerous books and pamphlets and publishes the annual newsletter *Lesbian and Gay Archivist.*

## Children of Lesbians and Gays Everywhere (COLAGE)
3543 Eighteenth St., #1, San Francisco, CA 94110
(415) 861-KIDS (5437) • fax: (415) 255-8345
Web site: www.colage.org/index.html

COLAGE is an international organization to support young people with gay, lesbian, bisexual, or transgendered parents. It coordinates pen pal and scholarship programs and sponsors an annual family week to celebrate family diversity. COLAGE publishes a quarterly newsletter and maintains several e-mail discussion lists.

## Citizens for Community Values (CCV)
11175 Reading Rd. Suite 103, Cincinnati, OH 45241
(513) 733-5775 • fax: (513) 733-5794
Web site: www.ccv.org

Citizens for Community Values exists to promote Judeo-Christian moral values and to reduce destructive behaviors contrary to those values through education, active community partnership, and individual empowerment at the local, state, and national levels. The CCV believes that gay and lesbian rights activism presents one of the greatest threats to traditional family values. It operates a speakers bureau and publishes the quarterly newsletter *Citizens' Courier.*

## Concerned Women for America (CWA)
1015 Fifteenth St. NW, Suite 1100, Washington, DC 20005
(202) 488-7000 • fax: (202) 488-0806
Web site: www.cwfa.org

The CWA is an educational and legal defense foundation that seeks to strengthen the traditional family by applying Judeo-Christian moral standards. It opposes gay marriage and the granting of additional civil rights protections to gays and lesbians. It publishes the monthly magazine *Family Voice* and various position papers on gay marriage and other issues.

**Equal Marriage for Same-Sex Couples**
Kevin Bourassa and Joe Varnell
c/o Bruce E. Walker Law Office
65 Wellesley St. East, Suite 205, Toronto, ON M4Y 1G7 Canada
(416) 961-7451
Web site: www.samesexmarriage.ca

Equal Marriage was started in 2001 by Kevin Bourassa and Joe Varnell when their Toronto Metropolitan Community Church went to court in Ontario, Canada, (with several same-sex couples) seeking government recognition of civil gay marriage. The organization acts as a clearinghouse of legal information about same-sex marriage in Canada and the United States. It also is a center for legal and social action, and it publishes an e-mail newsletter.

**Family Pride Coalition**
PO Box 65327, Washington, DC 20035
(202) 331-5015 • fax: (202) 331-0080
Web site: www.familypride.org

The coalition advocates for the well-being of lesbian, gay, bisexual and transgendered (LGBT) parents and their families through mutual support, community collaboration, and public understanding. It lobbies for positive public policy, educates communities about LGBT families, and provides information for LGBT families to enhance their lives. Family Pride publishes numerous pamphlets such as *How to Talk to Children About Our Families*, and the quarterly newsletter *Family Tree*.

**Family Research Council (FRC)**
801 G St. NW, Washington, DC 20001
(202) 393-2100 • fax: (202) 393-2134
Web site: www.frc.org

The council is a research and educational organization that promotes the traditional family, which the council defines as a group of people bound by marriage, blood, or adoption. The council opposes gay marriage and adoption rights. It publishes numerous reports from a conservative perspective on issues affecting the family, including *Free to Be Family*. Among its other publications are the monthly newsletters *State of the Family, Washington Watch,* and the semiannual journal *Family Policy Review*.

**Gay & Lesbian Alliance Against Defamation (GLAAD)**
248 W. Thirty-fifth St., 8th Fl., New York, NY 10001
(212) 629-3322 • fax: (212) 629-3225
Web site: www.glaad.org

GLAAD works to promote fair, accurate, and inclusive representation in the media as a means of eliminating homophobia and discrimination based on gender identity and sexual orientation. The organization publishes the online newsletters *GLAAD Alert* and *Calls to Action, a Media Reference Guide*, and training manuals to educate people about responsible and evenhanded media.

**Gay, Lesbian and Straight Education Network (GLSEN)**
121 W. Twenty-seventh St., Suite 804, New York, NY 10001
(212) 727-0135 • fax: (212) 727-0254
Web site: www.glsen.org

GLSEN is a national nonprofit organization that develops and implements policies to ensure safe schools for gay, lesbian, bisexual, and transgendered students and teachers. GLSEN conducts an annual conference and distributes Respect Awards to honor leaders who help to promote acceptance of all people in educational settings. The organization publishes articles such as "Is This the Right School for Us?" and curriculum guides, including "At Issue: Exploring the Debate over Marriage Rights for Same-Sex Couples" and "How Does Homophobia Hurt Us All?"

**Human Rights Campaign Foundation (HRC)**
1640 Rhode Island Ave. NW, Washington, DC 20036
(202) 628-4160
Web site: www.hrc.org

HRC is a clearinghouse of information for lesbian, gay, bisexual, and transgendered families coordinated by the Human Rights Campaign Foundation. It provides information and resources about adoption, gay marriage, civil unions, coming out, custody and visitation, donor insemination, family law, families of origin, marriage, money, parenting, religion, schools, senior health and housing, state laws and legislation, straight spouses, and transgender and workplace issues. HRC publishes numerous reports and the biweekly *HRC FamilyNet News.*

## Lambda Legal Defense and Education Fund
120 Wall St., Suite 1500, New York, NY 10005
(212) 809-8585 • fax: (212) 809-0055
Web site: www.lambdalegal.org

Lambda is a public interest law firm committed to achieving full recognition of the civil rights of lesbians, gay men, and people with HIV/AIDS. The firm addresses a variety of topics, including equal marriage rights, parenting and relationship issues, and domestic-partner benefits. It believes marriage is a basic right and an individual choice. Lambda publishes the quarterly *Lambda Update*, the pamphlet *Freedom to Marry*, and several position papers on same-sex marriage and gay and lesbian family rights.

## National Association for Research and Therapy of Homosexuality (NARTH)
16633 Ventura Blvd., Suite 1340, Encino, CA 91436-1801
(818) 789-4440 • fax: (818) 789-6452
Web site: www.narth.com

Founded in 1992 by former psychiatrist Charles W. Socarides, NARTH is a nonprofit organization dedicated to affirming a traditional heterosexual model of gender and sexuality. NARTH provides educational resources and a therapist referral to homosexuals who seek to become heterosexual. It publishes the newsletter *NARTH Bulletin* three times a year and distributes pamphlets and position papers such as *Sexual Politics and Scientific Logic: The Issues of Homosexuality* and *Homosexual Advocacy Groups & Your School*.

## Parents, Friends, and Family of Lesbians and Gays (P-FLAG)
1726 M St. NW, Suite 400, Washington, DC 20036
(202) 467-8180 • fax: (202) 467-8194
Web site: www.pflag.org

P-FLAG is a national organization that provides support and education services for gays, lesbians, bisexuals, transgendered people, and their families and friends. It also works to end prejudice and discrimination against homosexuals. It publishes and distributes pamphlets and articles, including *Faith in Our Families; Our Daughters and Sons: Questions and Answers for Parents of Gay, Lesbian, Bisexual, and Transgendered People*; and *Hate Crimes Hurt Families.*

 **For Further Research**

## Books

Sidney Abbott and Barbara Love, *Sappho Was a Right-On Woman*. New York: Stein and Day, 1972.

Adam D. Barry, *The Rise of a Gay and Lesbian Movement*. Rev. ed. New York: Twayne, 1995.

Mary Bernstein and Renate Reimann, eds., *Queer Families, Queer Politics: Challenging Culture and the State*. New York: Columbia University Press, 2001.

Mark Blasius and Shane Phelan, *We Are Everywhere: A Historical Sourcebook of Gay and Lesbian Politics*. New York: Routledge, 1997.

Christopher Bull and John Gallagher, *Perfect Enemies: The Religious Right, the Gay Movement, and the Politics of the 1990s*. New York: Crown, 1996.

James W. Button, Barbara A. Rienzo, and Kenneth D. Wald, *Private Lives, Public Conflicts: Battles over Gay Rights in American Communities*. Washington, DC: CQ, 1997.

Patricia Cain, *Rainbow Rights: The Role of Lawyers and Courts in the Lesbian and Gay Civil Rights Movement*. Boulder, CO: Westview, 2001.

Dudley Clendinen and Adam Nagourney, *Out for Good: The Struggle to Build a Gay Rights Movement in America*. New York: Simon & Schuster, 1999.

John D'Emilio, *Sexual Politics, Sexual Communities: The Making of a Homosexual Minority in the United States, 1940–1970*. Chicago: University of Chicago Press, 1998.

John D'Emilio and Estelle Freedman, *Intimate Matters: A His-*

*tory of Sexuality in America.* New York: Harper and Row, 1988.

Martin Duberman, *Stonewall.* New York: Dutton, 1993.

Martin Duberman, Martha Vicinus, and George Chauncey Jr., eds., *Hidden from History: Reclaiming the Gay and Lesbian Past.* New York: Meridian, 1989.

William N. Eskridge Jr., *Gay Law: Challenging the Apartheid of the Closet.* Cambridge, MA: Harvard University Press, 1999.

Lillian Faderman, *Odd Girls and Twilight Lovers: A History of Lesbian Life in Twentieth-Century America.* New York: Columbia University Press, 1991.

George E. Haggerty, ed., *Gay Histories and Cultures: An Encyclopedia.* New York: Garland, 2000.

Mark Hertzog, *The Lavender Vote: Lesbians, Gay Men, and Bisexuals in American Electoral Politics.* New York: New York University Press, 1996.

Lisa Keen and Suzanne Goldberg, *Strangers to the Law: Gay People on Trial.* Ann Arbor: University of Michigan Press, 1998.

Elizabeth Kennedy and Madeline Davis, *Boots of Leather, Slippers of Gold: The History of a Lesbian Community.* New York: Routledge, 1993.

Eric Marcus, *Making History: The Struggle for Gay and Lesbian Equal Rights 1945–1990.* New York: HarperCollins, 1992.

Toby Marotta, *The Politics of Homosexuality.* Boston: Houghton Mifflin, 1981.

David McWhirter, Stephanie Sanders, and June Machover Reinisch, eds., *Homosexuality/Heterosexuality: Concepts of Sexual Orientation.* New York: Oxford University Press, 1990.

Neil Miller, *Out of the Past: Gay and Lesbian History from 1869 to the Present.* New York: Vintage, 1995.

Joyce Murdoch and Deb Price, *Courting Justice: Gay Men and Lesbians v. the Supreme Court.* New York: Basic Books, 2001.

Joan Nestle, *The Persistent Desire: A Fem-Butch Reader.* Boston: Alyson, 1992.

Saul M. Olyan and Martha C. Nussbaum, eds., *Sexual Orientation and Human Rights in American Religious Discourse.* New York: Oxford University Press, 1998.

David Rayside, *On the Fringe: Gays and Lesbians in Politics.* Ithaca, NY: Cornell University Press, 1998.

Craig A. Rimmerman, Kenneth D. Wald, and Clyde Wilcox, eds., *The Politics of Gay Rights.* Chicago: University of Chicago Press, 2000.

Randy Shilts, *And the Band Played On: People, Politics, and the AIDS Epidemic.* New York: St. Martin's, 1987.

———, *Conduct Unbecoming: Gays and Lesbians in the U.S. Military.* New York: St. Martin's, 1993.

———, *The Mayor of Castro Street: The Life and Times of Harvey Milk.* New York: St. Martin's, 1982.

Urvashi Vaid, *Virtual Equality: The Mainstreaming of Gay and Lesbian Liberation.* New York: Anchor, 1995.

Michael Warner, The *Trouble with Normal: Sex, Politics, and the Ethics of Queer Life.* New York: Free Press, 1999.

Stephanie L. Witt and Suzanne McCorkle, *Anti-Gay Rights: Assessing Voter Initiatives.* Westport, CT: Praeger, 1997.

Bonnie Zimmerman, ed., *Lesbian Histories and Cultures: An Encyclopedia.* New York: Garland, 2000.

———, *The Safe Sea of Women: Lesbian Fiction 1969–1989.* Boston: Beacon, 1990.

# Periodicals

Marcus Baram, "The Two Sides of Stonewall Raise Glasses on Common Ground," *New York Times*, June 27, 2004.

John M. Broder, "Groups Debate Slower Strategy on Gay Rights," *New York Times*, December 9, 2004.

Dudley Clendinen, "Gay, Middle-Aged and Still Militant," *New York Times*, May 2, 2000.

———, "Harry Hay, Early Proponent of Gay Rights, Dies at 90," *New York Times*, October 25, 2002.

John Cloud, "The New Face of Gay Power," *Time*, October 13, 2003.

———, "Standing Up for Gay Rights," *Time*, March 31, 2003.

Robert Dreyfuss, "Pride and Prejudice," *Rolling Stone*, May 25, 2000.

James Driscoll, "New Gay Political Strategies," *Washington Times*, November 18, 2004.

Martin Duberman, "Uncloseted History," *Nation*, June 14, 1999.

Victor Dwyer, "Not So Queer as Folk," *Maclean's*, June 23, 2003.

Jeremy Kinser, "Stonewall 30," *Advocate*, June 22, 1999.

Stanley N. Kurtz, "Civil Revolt," *National Review*, October 9, 2000.

Tamar Lewin, "The Gay Rights Movement, Settled Down," *New York Times*, February 29, 2004.

Gregory B. Lewis, "Black-White Differences in Attitudes Toward Homosexuality and Gay Rights," *Public Opinion Quarterly*, Spring 2003.

Scott McLemee, "A Queer Notion of History," *Chronicle of Higher Education*, September 12, 2003.

Stephen O. Murray, "Tracing the Rise of the Gay Rights Movement," *New York Times*, July 5, 1999.

Lisa Neff, "History Makers," *Advocate*, January 21, 2003.

*New York Times*, "Black Ministers Protest Gay Marriage," March 23, 2004.

*New York Times*, "Gay Rights Movement Said to Reach a Critical Moment," August 10, 2003.

Achy Obejas and Julia Lieblich, "Ex-gay Movement Works to Change Sexual Orientation," *Chicago Tribune*, August 7, 2001.

Karen Ocamb, "Lesbian Pioneer Betty Berzon," *Lesbian News*, May 2004.

Justin Raimondo, "A Gay Man Decries 'Gay Rights,'" *American Enterprise*, March 2000.

Marisa Robertson-Textor, "A One-Man Gay Rights Movement," *Advocate*, March 2, 2004.

Walter Shapiro, "Advances in Gay Rights Overtake Health Policy," *USA Today*, May 19, 2004.

Kenneth Sherill, "The Political Power of Lesbians, Gays, and Bisexuals," *Political Science and Politics*, September 1996.

Melody Sias, "Birthplace of Gay-Rights Movement Now a National Historic Landmark," *Knight Ridder Tribune*, March 15, 2000.

Michelangelo Signorile, "A Journey Through Our Gay Century," *Advocate*, January 18, 2000.

Stuart Taylor Jr., "Gay Marriage Isn't an Issue for the Courts to Decide," November 22, 2003.

*Toronto Star*, "Sodomy Laws Face Review in U.S.," December 3, 2002.

*USA Today*, "Same Sex Marriage Top Priority for Gays," June 19, 2002.

Debbie Woodell, "Here Are Some Additional Heroes of the Gay Rights Movement," *Philadelphia Daily News*, January 21, 2000.

## Internet Sources

Brett Beemyn, "Marches on Washington," *glbtq: An Encyclopedia of Gay, Lesbian, Bisexual, Transgender and Queer Culture*, April 18, 2005. http://www.glbtq.com/social-sci ences/marches_washington.html.

Vern Bullough, "When Did the Gay Rights Movement Begin?" *History News Network*, April 18, 2005. http://hnn.us/articles/11316.html.

John Cloud, "The Battle Over Gay Marriage," *Time*, February 16, 2004. http://www.time.com/time/archive/preview/0,10987,993370,00.html.

Steve Hartman, "Hartman: Gay Rights in America," CBS News, March 3, 2004. http://www.cbsnews.com/stories /2004/03/03/60II/.

Ramon Johnson, "The History of Gay Rights," About.com, 2005. http://gaylife.about.com/od/gayrights/a/history rights.

Knitting Circle Lesbian and Gay Staff Association of London South Bank University, "Timetable of Lesbian and Gay History," February 20, 2005. http://myweb.lsbu.ac.uk/ ~stafflag/timetable.html.

Rictor Norton, "Taking a 'Husband': A History of Gay Marriage," Gay History and Literature, February 2004. www.infopt.demon.co.uk/marriage.htm.

Charles Edward Riffenburg IV, "Symbols of the Gay, Lesbian, Bisexual, and Transgender Movements," December 26, 2004. http://www.lambda.org/symbols.htm.

Leila J. Rupp, "Lesbian Organizations," *Reader's Compan-*

*ion to U.S Women's History*, 2004. http://college.hmco.
com/history/readerscomp/women/html/wh-021000-les
bianorgan.htm.

David Von Drehle, "Gay Marriage Enters the American Consciousness," MSNBC, November 22, 2003. http://www.
msnbc.msn.com/id/3540727.